Georges Bernage

The Battle of Normandy The guide

HEIMDAL

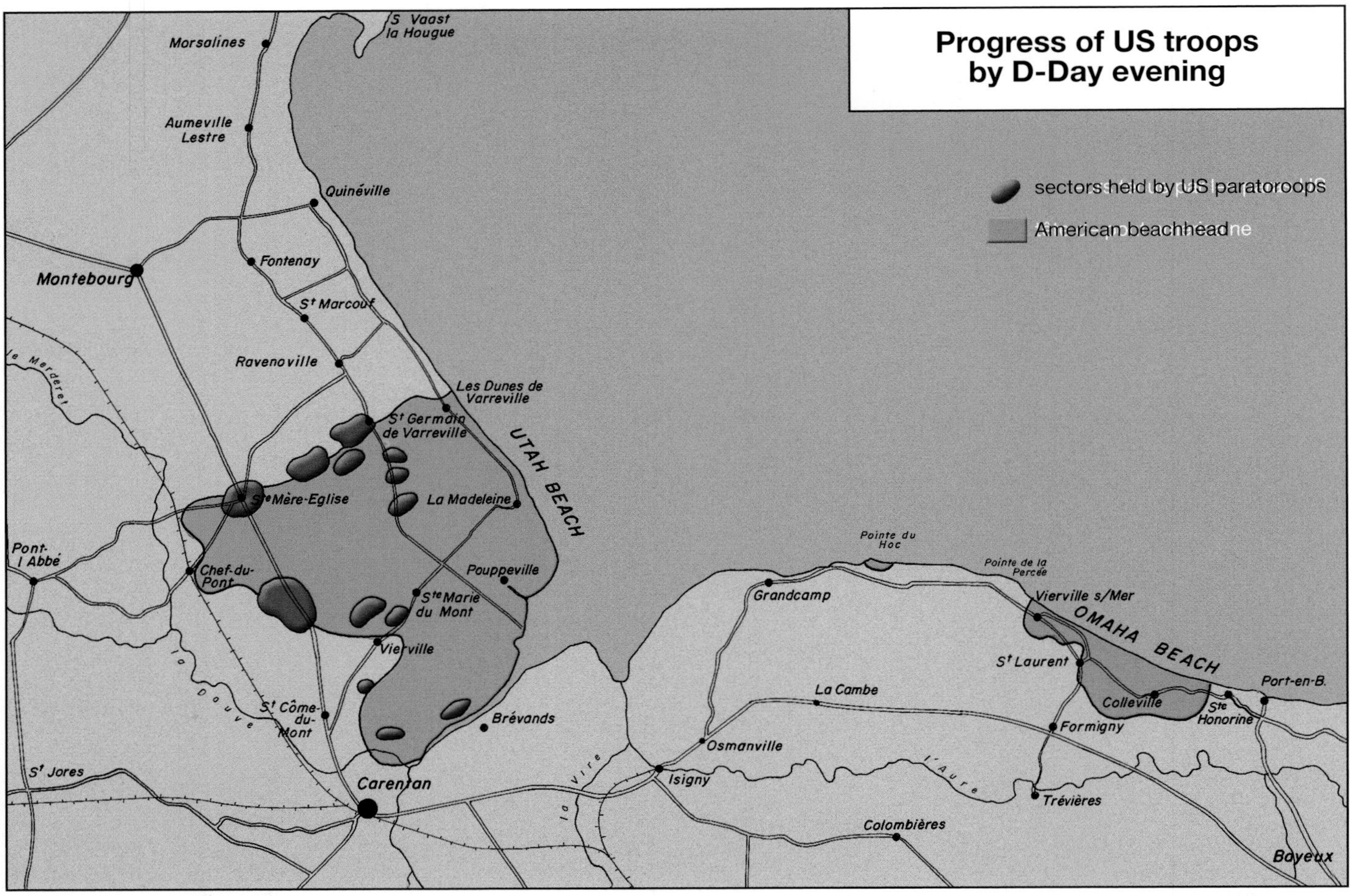

Progress of US troops by D-Day evening

sectors held by US paratoroops
American beachhead

Morsalines
S Vaast la Hougue
Aumeville Lestre
Quinéville
Montebourg
Fontenay
St Marcouf
Ravenoville
Les Dunes de Varreville
St Germain de Varreville
UTAH BEACH
Ste Mère-Eglise
La Madeleine
Pont-l Abbé
Chef-du-Pont
Pouppeville
Ste Marie du Mont
Vierville
St Côme-du-Mont
Brévands
St Jores
Carentan
Pointe du Hoc
Pointe de la Percée
Grandcamp
Vierville s/Mer
OMAHA BEACH
St Laurent
Colleville
Ste Honorine
Port-en-B.
La Cambe
Formigny
Osmanville
Isigny
Trévières
Colombières
Bayeux

June 7th, daybreak on the Allied bridgeheads

Rommel's plan was to repel the Allied invasion back into the sea ; This is the reason why he fortified the Atlantic wall, though a bit too late and not enough. The plan worked relatively well on rough sectors such as behind Omaha Beach where the american landings almost ended up in disaster. On the other hand, on Utah Beach, the flat land, levelled by heavy bombings showed very little german resistance, and even the marshes proved no obstacle to the invading force. And in this particular sector, the advance of the 4th Infantry Division was greatly facilitated by the airborne operations on the night of june 5th. However, the 82nd and 101st Airborne divisions do not hold a continuous front line. They mostly occupy strong points in the middle of a large zone where German and Georgian soldiers are still fighting.The Omaha Beach head is even narrower and has cost the Americans dearly. The Rangers are still surrounded at the Pointe du Hoc. Trévières, in the south, should have been reached, along with Isigny. The two american bridgeheads will have to connect around Carentan as discussed later.

The anglo-canadian beach head is the larger one. To the east, the 6th Airborne Division and the Commandos have established a bridge head east of the Orne river offering an escape way across the river and the canal. But north of Caen, the 3rd British Infantry Division has not reached its objectives, stuck north of Lebisey by elements of the 21.Panzer-Division. Caen, a D Day objective cannot be liberated. It will take a whole month to conquer a ruined city. Furthermore, elements of the 21.PD have broken through to the sea, in the Luc sur Mer area preventing the link up with the canadian beach head. Regarding the

A 105 mm HM2 Howitzer on a « Priest » chassis fires away. These artillery pieces on armored chassis allowed great speed in combat. (DAVA/Heimdal)

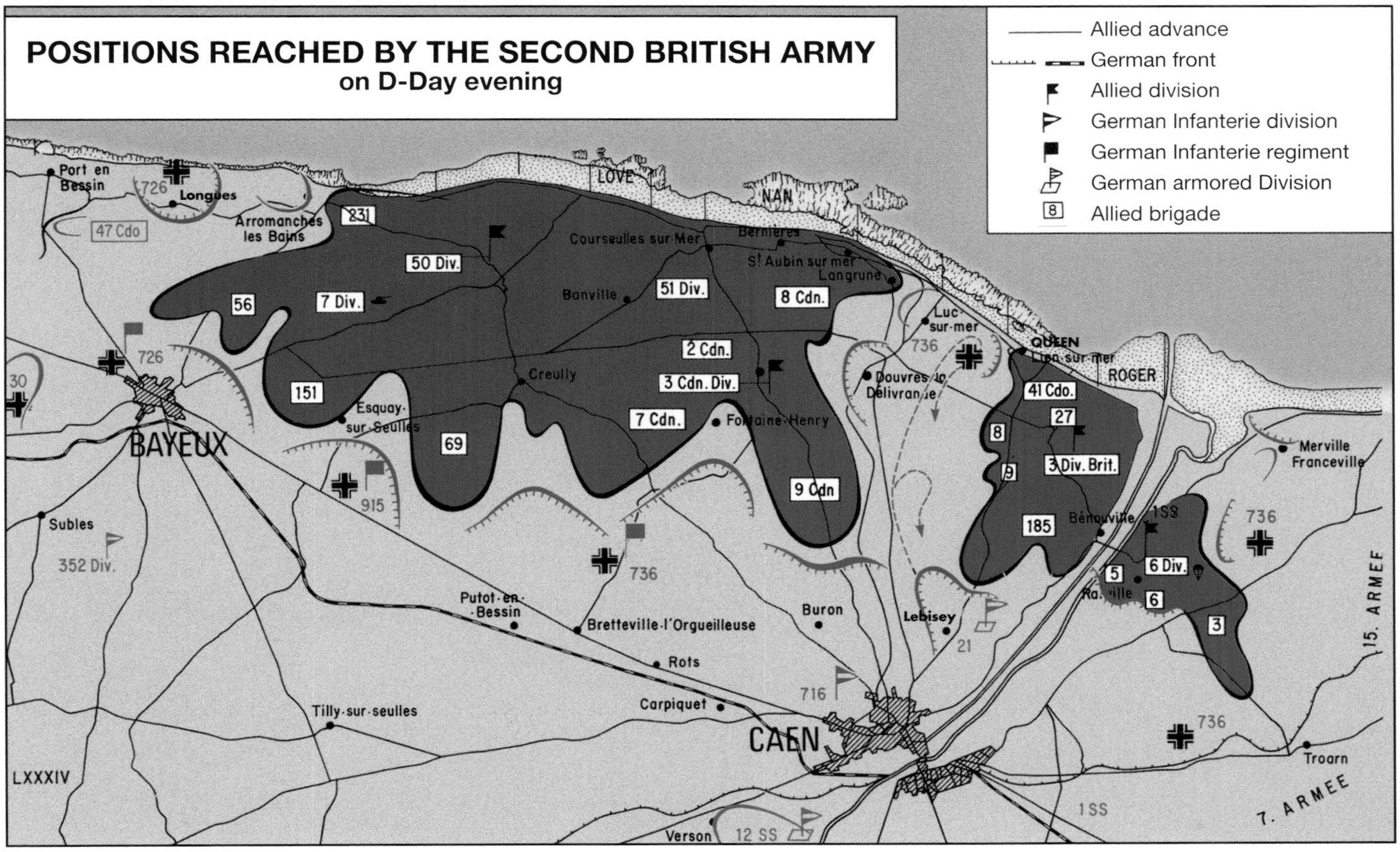

POSITIONS REACHED BY THE SECOND BRITISH ARMY
on D-Day evening

Allied advance
German front
Allied division
German Infanterie division
German Infanterie regiment
German armored Division
Allied brigade

strong radar base in Douvres-la-Delivrande, although surrounded, it will hold many more days, providing the German High Command with valuable informations on British troop movements in the area.

In the center, the 3rd Canadian Infantry Division, in spite of quite a traffic jam to exit the beaches, has made the greatest advance on D Day. Its 9th Brigade has moved on north of Buron and environs for June 7th the taking of Carpiquet airfield and the west of Caen.

Further west, the British 50th Infantry Division closes in on Bayeux ; some patrols enter the town in the evening. It is in this area that the link up with the American bech head at Omaha must be secured. It is noteworthy that in this area, the 50th British ID and a Canadian division have made good progresses, taking advantage of weak and scattered 716. Infanterie-Division elements, when the 3rd British Division faced the 21. Panzer-Division in the Caen area. To successfully push back the Allies into the sea would have required panzer divisions and only one was available. More are rushing to the front. The 12. SS-Panzer-Division « Hitlerjugend » just arrived in the Caen sector.

Rare color photograph of a Hitlerjugend grenadier. The German soldiers will offer stiff resistance, inflicting heavy casualties to the Allies who will not breakthrough the front lines until the end of July. The battle of Normandy will be a costly affair. (Coll. Heimdal.)

21st Army Group headquarters in Creullet, early June. From left to right, Sir Alan Brooke, Imperial Chief of staff, Winston Churchill, General Bernard L. Montgomery. (IWM).

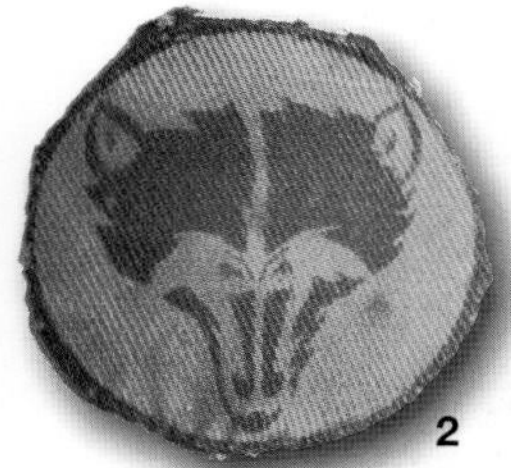

2

1

3

4

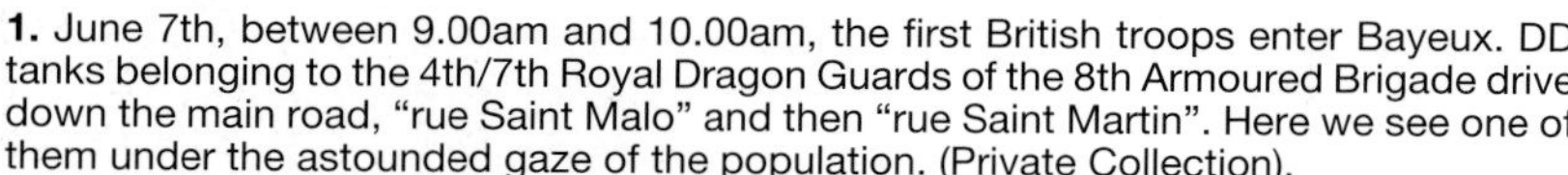

1. June 7th, between 9.00am and 10.00am, the first British troops enter Bayeux. DD tanks belonging to the 4th/7th Royal Dragon Guards of the 8th Armoured Brigade drive down the main road, "rue Saint Malo" and then "rue Saint Martin". Here we see one of them under the astounded gaze of the population. (Private Collection).

2. Cloth emblem of the 8th Armoured Brigade, sewn on the top of the sleeve of members belonging to this unit. (Private Collection).

3 and **4.** Crossroads in the hamlet "Douet de Chouain", on the road going from Bayeux to Tilly. A Bren Gun Carrier makes its way back to Bayeux (photo taken on the 13th) and drives past one of the three Dingos that were lost on June 7th. In the present photo, we can recognize a few houses which were not destroyed. (IWM and S. Jacquet).

5 and **6.** Juaye-Mondaye, at the "ferme des Pallieres" (Pallieres farm) on June 9th in the morning. A Panther tank belonging to the 2nd company of the tank regiment of the Panzer-Lehr-Division and an Sd.Kfz 251/9 fitted with a short 75mm gun prepare to attack towards Bayeux; they were not to go much further. (ECPAD and S. Jacquet).

7. Outside the "ferme des Pallieres", team leaders of the Panzer-Lehr-Division gather to study the progress they have made on the map. Some of them belong to the division's reconnaissance group, the Pz.A.L.A.130. The man you can see on the right may be Lieutenant Gerstenmeier from the 3rd company. The name of the Panther in the background is "Hesla".

8. MK II helmet with the insignia of the XXX Corps. (Private Collection).

9. MK II helmet with the insignia of the 50th ID. (Private Collection).

10. Helmet and its helmet cover, worn by the grenadiers of the PLD. (Private Collection).

Bayeux sector

On June 6th in the evening, the 2nd British Army's anglo-canadian sector, including the XXX Corps (50th Northumbrian Infantry Division) to the west, and the Ist Corps (3rd Canadian Infantry Division, 3rd British Infantry Division and the 6th Airborne Division) in the center and to the east, form a wide beachhead between the eastern side of Bayeux, and the the east bank of the Orne River. The tough Canadian Division has almost reached all of its objectives. The same can be said of the 50th Division that reached Bayeux out of Gold Beach.On the other hand, the 3rd British Division stalled in front of Caen and could not join up with the Canadians.

On wednesday June 7th, the 50th Northumbrian Division pours into Bayeux in the early hours. The city picked to be a rest area is intact. On Thursday June 8th, Port en Bessin is clear of ennemy after two days of fighting by the N°47 Royal Marine Commando that link up in the evening with US troops of the 1st Infantry Division. To the south, the 50th Division backed by 210 tanks of the 8th Armoured Brigade moved up towards Tilly sur Seules and Villers Bocage. By nightfall, a tactical group lead by tanks has achieved a 9 kimometers penetration, reaching Hill 103 and the hamlet of Saint Pierre, north east from Tilly sur Seules. But on the 9th, this group is engaged by the first elements of the Panzer-Lehr-Division. Panther tanks reach Ellon by midday, and Arganchy at 1.00 pm, 5 km from Bayeux. It takes Allied naval artillery to stop them.

6

5

8

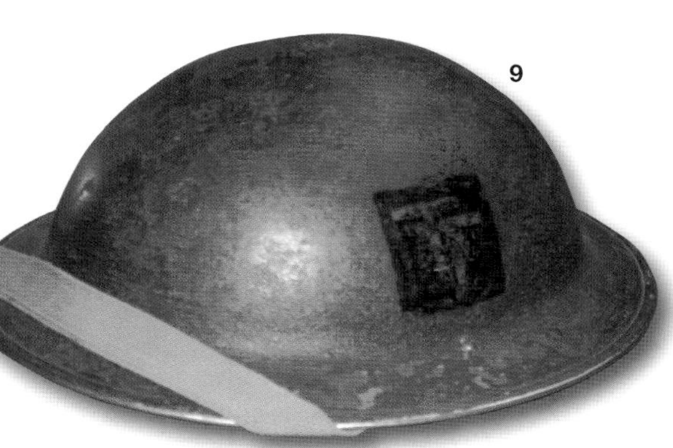
9

10

7

On June 8th and 9th, the Dorset and tanks from 4/7 Dragoon Guards link up near Hill 103 with tanks from the Sherwood Rangers. Then on the 8th, Durham seizes Saint Pierre (North east from Tilly) with the help from 24 Lancers. The Panzer-Lehr-Division fails in its attempt to occupy Bayeux, but stops the British cold in front of Tilly. A terrible battle is about to rage for a full month.

June 7th-10th

Canadians against Hitlerjugend

1. Panther tank knocked out on Bretteville l'Orgueilleuse main Heighway (RN13) during the fierce fighting in the night of june 8th . Rear sight view of the wreckage. The turret has been blown off from the rear by a shell fired inadvertendly by another Panther tank. This was the first Panther destroyed in Normandy.More would be knocked out the following night south of town. (IWM)

2. Nowadays. (E. Groult/Heimdal)

3. After the Norrey battle, the main german leaders gather at La Villeneuve, part of Rots, to assess the situation. From left to right, unidentified officer (back), Max Wünsche (bandaged head, as he got hit during the night fighting), Bernhard Krause (I/26 CO), italian camouflage pattern jacket with special rank insignia, and Kurt Meyer. (Coll. Heimdal)

4. Late morning june 9th, grenadiers from the HitlerJugend 15./25 return to La Villeneuve de Rots following the repulse of the attack on Norrey. (Coll Heimdal).

5. Same place but looking south and the RN 13 highway. A Panther from 3rd Company is parked after the Norrey assault. The tank commander of N° 326 is KIA. (Coll. G.B.)

7. Emblem painted on vehicles belongingto the 12thSS-Panzer-Division"HitlerJugend".

8. Emblem of the Regina,the Canadian regiment that defended Bretteville and Norrey.

On June 6th, Canadian troops of the 3rd Division had accomplished most of their objectives, right after pushing through the costal defenses where they suffered heavy casualties. Beyond a thin coastal defensive line, the Germans no longer had serious reserves to oppose to the advancing Canadians. Things will change on june 7th when the 12. SS-Panzer-Division « Hitlerjugend » moves up to the front to fight them off. So it is in the early hours of June 7th when the 9th Canadian Brigade advances west of Caen to cross the RN 13 and take Carpiquet airfield. It comes under attack on its flank by panzers from the « Hitlerjugend » coming out of the « Abbaye d'Ardenne » that crushes its front lines : it will take the canadians a full month to overrun Carpiquet at the price of horrendous losses. Meanwhile, the « Hitlerjugend » still wants to push the Canadians back into the sea. The Germans counter attack with a Combat Team, Kampfgruppe Meyer-Wünsche, in the evening of June 8th. They fail, and Panther tanks are set afire inside Bretteville-l'Orgueilleuse ans its surroundings. Canadian riflemen of the Winnipeg have in the mean time suffered heavy casualties at Putot (West of Bretteville) on the 8th. The fighting is brutal, and prisonners are being executed on both sides, Germans from the PLD, and Canadians at Authie, Ardenne, Audrieu and Mesnil-Patry. On June 9th, the Hitlerjugend leads a new counter attack, using Panther tanks from Ribbentrop's company in the Norrey sector. Once again, it's a failure. The front, so unstable these last few days, finally comes to a stanstill between two ruthless ennemies both suffering terrible losses.

Further to the east, and following the British 3rd Division's failure, the front stabilizes for a month north of Caen. East of the Orne river, British paratroopers from the 6th Airborne Division are also stuck within their beachhead facing Kampfgruppe Luck.

As the situation develops on June 10th, English and Canadians appear to have come to a stanstill inside a narrow beachhead running west to east ; the British, with tanks and the 50th Division stuck in front the Panzer-Lehr-Division, and the British 3rd Division and 6th Airborne Division blocked facing Caen, and east of the Orne by the 21. Panzer-Division.

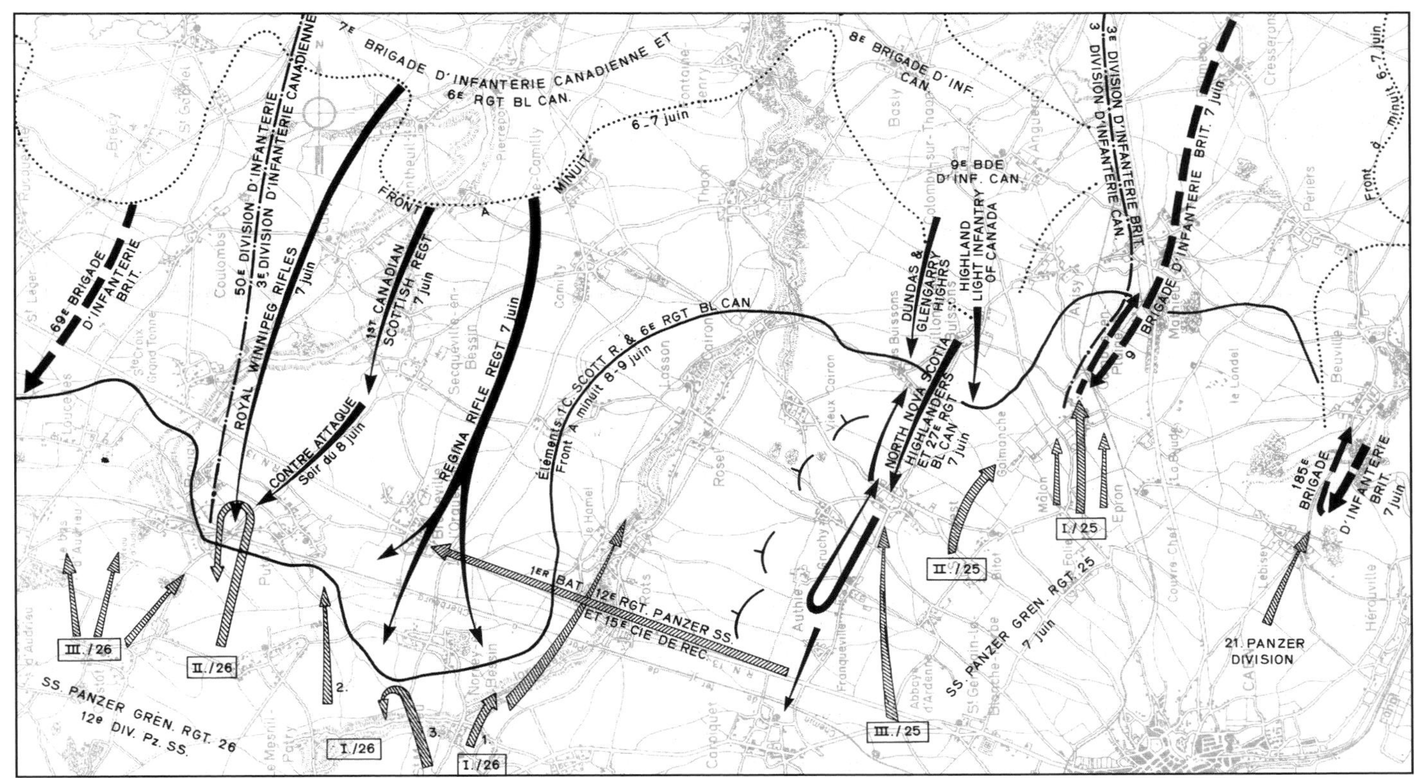

This map sums up the movements of the 3rd Canadian Infantry Division on June 7th 1944. It appears that the Regina Rifle Regiment accomplished the deepest penetration, all the way to Norrey en Bessin. The dotted line shows the position on June 6th in the morning and the straight line the positions in the evening. On the right flank is the RWR. The third unit of the 7th Brigade, the first Canadian Scottish is in reserve to the rear and will support the RWR on June 8th. Facing them are units of Mohnke's SS-Panzer-grenadier-Regiment 26. This regiment and the 7th Brigade are of equal strength. From the east (on the left side) comes the 9th Brigade en route to a bloody failure. Its attack is repulsed far back all the way to its line of departure and away from Carpiquet (on the left side of the map). The Novas are pushed back by the III./25 and the HLI by the II./25. The I./25 repulses another 9th Brigade, the one belonging to the British 3rd Division. (Heimdal map).

6. One of the Panther tank knocked out close to Norrey in the morning of June 9th. To the south runs the railroad track, visible on the left hand side of the picture.

June 7th-10th

29th Infantry Division.

From Omaha Beach

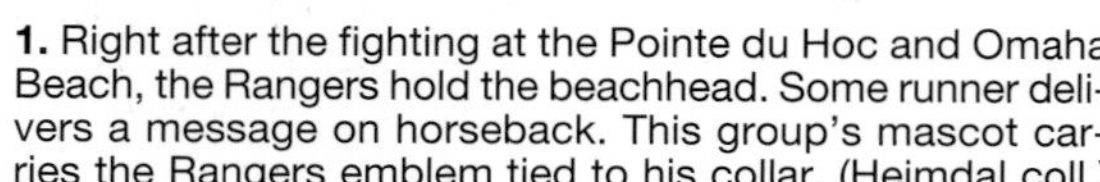

1. Right after the fighting at the Pointe du Hoc and Omaha Beach, the Rangers hold the beachhead. Some runner delivers a message on horseback. This group's mascot carries the Rangers emblem tied to his collar. (Heimdal coll.)

2. An american half track drives in front of Isigny church whose bell tower has been shelled. As the story goes, german snipers were using it. (DAVA.)

3 and **4.** Isigny central place looking east ; in the background is the road to Bayeux. An MP is regulating traffic. Rubbles have been partly removed after the civilian population returned. Hotel still exists. (NA & EG/Heimdal.)

5 and **6.** Trévières. This picture was shot on june 15th on the market place facing Hotel Saint Aignan spared from destruction. The body of a german soldier lies there abandonned 5 days after the fighting. (DAVA & EG/Heimdal.)

While in the west, General Joseph L Collins'VII Corps reinforces the bridgehead in the Cotentin Peninsula, and starts expanding its lines to the north (Montebourg then Cherbourg), west (Pont l'Abbé and the west coast) and east (Carentan), V Corps (Major General Leonard T Gerow commanding) created a new and quite narrow bridgehead on the high grounds over Omaha Beach on the evening of June 6th. Next day, June 7th, the sector broadens, thanks to the 1st Infantry Division towards Bayeux and Trévières, and to the 29th Infantry Division mainly towards the Pointe du Hoc, still isolated. On June 8th, the advance is more obvious towards the west, where the Pointe du Hoc is cleared of ennemy, while the 3rd Battalion, 175th Infantry regiment (29th Inf Division) closes on Isigny. To the east, and in the evening, a link up is achieved with British forces in the Bayeux area. The bridgehead has been expanded to the south all the way to the RN 13. On june 9th, Isigny is on fire following heavy bombing by the Navy. The little town is stormed by 2/175 and 3/175 supported by tanks from the 747th Tank Battalion. Isigny is liberated and over 200 Prisonners are taken. To the west, the bridge over the Vire river is destroyed. To the south, four more bridges have been destroyed over the Aure. The Engineers set one up and the Colombières sector is reached at 10.15 in the morning. The 115 RCT (29th ID) rushes south, in spite of heavy counter attacks by self propelled Marder (Pz.Jaeger-Abt. 358). The 175 RCT secures the western flank of the push, supported to the east by the 38th RCT (2nd Infantry division), that makes it to Trévières around midnight. By june 10th, all missions are accomplished, and the 115 RCT reaches Sainte Marguerite d'Elle, north east from Saint Lô. But the 352. Infanterie-Division sets up a new line of resis-

7 and **8.** Less than 15 kilometers fron Trévières, south and west from Littry, next to the oratorium, a 4,7 cm Pak (t) Panzer-Kampfwagen 35 R (f) has been abandonned. It is made of a czech anti tank gun mounted on a french Renault body; quite a combination. It belonged to the Schnelle-Abteilung 517. Picture taken by Moran on june 20th. The location is unchanged. Bernard Paich shot the recent picture in february 2004.

tance along the Elle river. Further east, the 9th IR (2nd Infantry Division) speeds through the Cerisy forest and reaches Balleroy in the evening. A threat is looming though ; the 17. SS-Panzergrenadier-Division « Götz von Berlichingem » is closing in. One tough ennemy approaching !

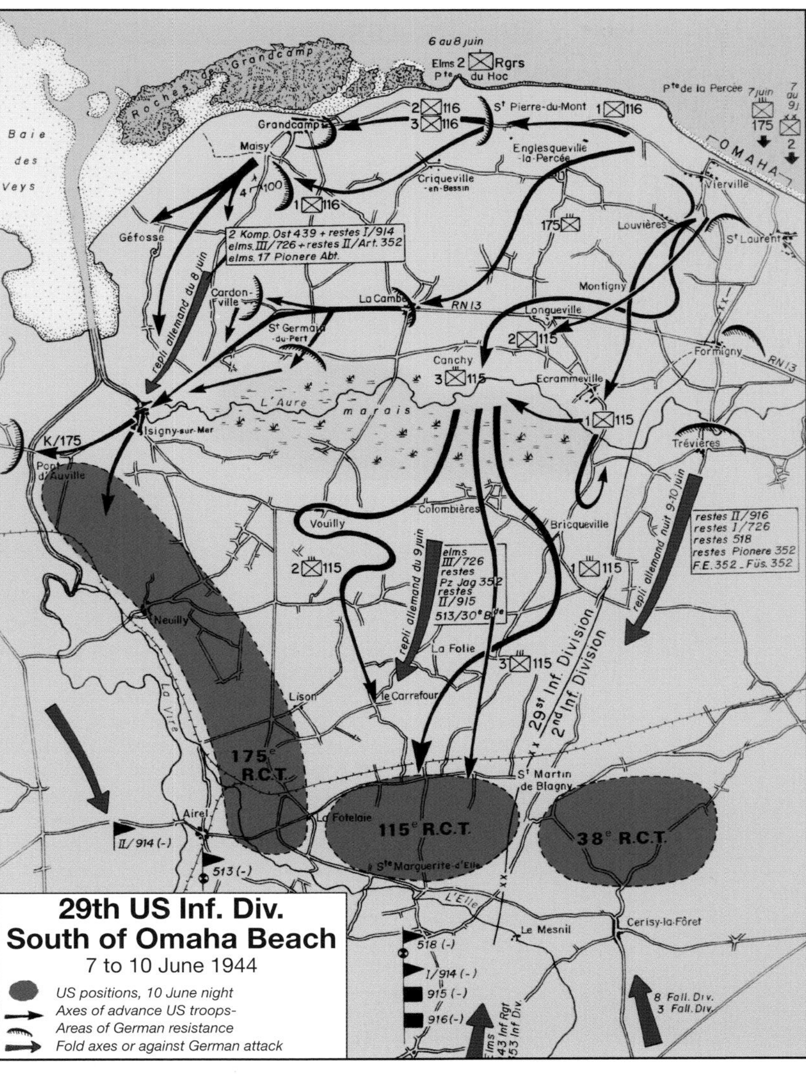

This map shows the fast advance made between June 7th and June 10th south of Omaha, beyond the marshy area of the Aure valley, the taking of Isigny and Trévières and the establishment of a front line along the Elle and Vire valleys, as previously planned. (Heimdal)

101st Airborne Division

1. Major von der Heydte' s FJ Reg 6 Command Post staged in Maison Marie at Dead Man's corner (now a museum). This historical dwelling is located above the crossroad and the Carentan causeway. (F. Coune/Heimdal.)

2. The church in Saint Côme du Mont. The bell tower, knocked down in 1944 has been totally rebuilt. F. Coune/Heimdal.)

3. The « maison Marie » in 1944, shown from the south end and the Carentan causeway. On the right end side on the Sainte Marie du Mont road, where the attack came from, (see map) stands the wrecked light tank belonging to D Company, 70th Tank Battalion knocked out by a German paratrooper from 6/6, Bruno Hinz. It is this wreckage and the exposed body of the tank commander lying across the turret that had the place called Dead man's corner. To the left (facing), the road from Sainte Mère Eglise and Saint Côme du Mont. (Coll. Centre Historique des Paras du Jour J)

Objective : Carentan

To the west, the Cotentin peninsula is a major objective, to consolidate the bridgehead and secure a deep sea harbor, Cherbourg. Two American Airborne divisions have jumped to the south east of the peninsula during the night of june 5th. The 82nd Airborne seized Sainte Mère eglise on the RN 13 between Cherbourg and Carentan, and must secure the La Fière causeway on the Merderet further west, and open the road to Cherbourg to the north. The 101st Airborne cleared the four exits leading to Utah Beach, where the 4th Infantry division landed with few casualties. The « screaming eagles » have been ordered to open the way to Carentan, across the Douve river and the inundated marshlands. German units in the area are being crushed under the power of these two airborne divisions and the seaborne infantry division. However, the 101st AB is facing an elite regiment south of its sector, Major von der Heydte's parachutists of the Fallschirmjaeger- Regiment 6. An indian warfare takes place in hedgerow country, opposing in fierce battle german and american parachutists until the fall of « Dead man's corner » in Saint Côme du Mont on June 8th. The 502nd PIR then advances on the Carentan causeway in order to link up with troops coming out of Omaha, and connect the two american beach heads.

4. German road sign still standing at the entrance of Saint Come now in the hands of paratroopers from the 101st Airborne. (Coll. Centre Historique des Paras du Jour J)

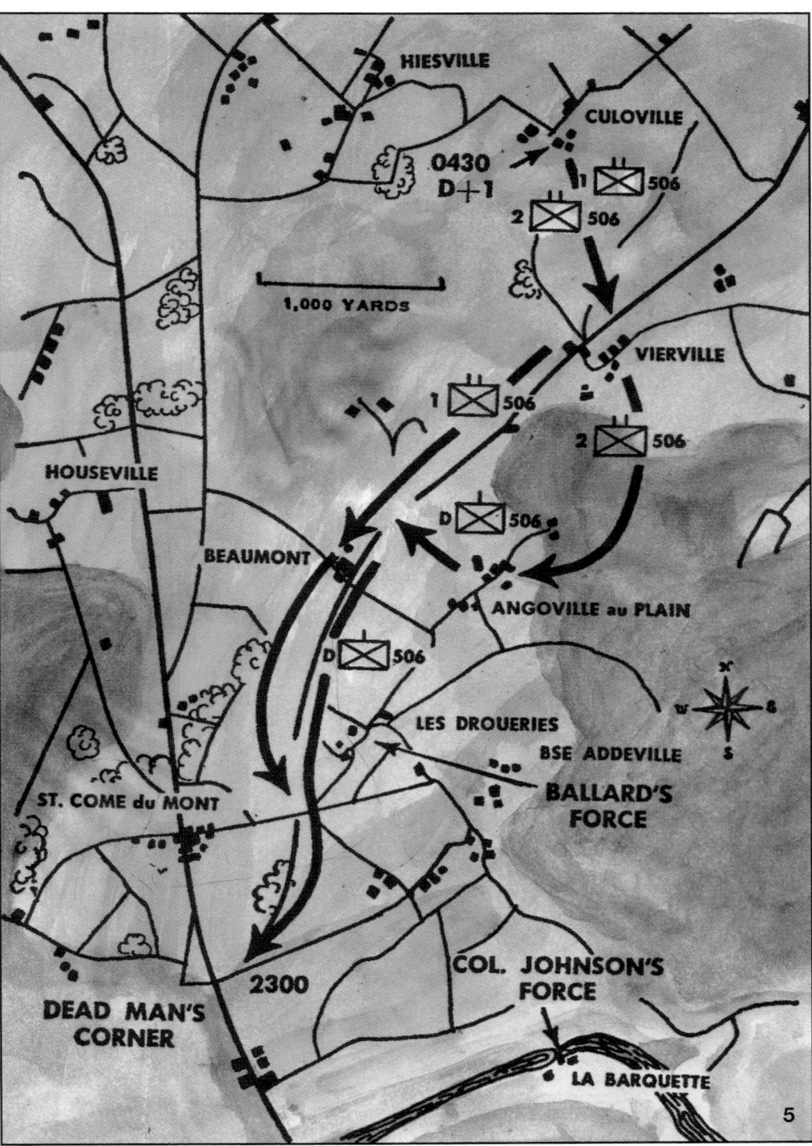

5. This map shows the advance of units from the 506th PIR towards Saint Côme du Mont on june 7th on Ballard's force sideway. Also shown is Colonel Johnson's force at the La Barquette locks. (Gen. Marshall/Heimdal.)

6. This aerial photo taken after most of the water dried out shows the La barquette locks and the high grounds above inundated areas to the North West ; Saint Côme du Mont is on the background to the left. (Coll. Centre Historique des Paras du Jour J)

7. The La barquette locks nowadays, looking towards the Douve River mouth. Colonel Johnson's positions were to the left. (EG/Heimdal.)

1. Troops coming from Utah Beach walking by the Sainte Marie du Mont church. Picture shot on June 7th by war correspondant Kaye (Coll. Heimdal).

2. This photo dated June 7th and depicting the Sainte Mère Eglise church is captionned : « American riflemen shooting at German snipers hidden in the steeple. » The Germans abandonned town in the early hours of June 6th and the first Americans into town were paratroopers. (Coll. Heimdal.)

3. Two american soldiers on the Sainte Mère Eglise market place about to search Jules Lemenicier hardware store (Coll. Heimdal.)

4. June 7th : American paratroopers have requisitionned horses and patrol Saint Mère Eglise downtown streets. (Coll. Heimdal.)

5. Now and then, the town practically untouched. (E.G./Heimdal.)

82nd Airborne shoulder insignia

Sainte Mère Eglise and La Fière

The two towns within the American beach head, Sainte Marie du Mont, on the 4th Infantry Division line of advance from the shore, and Sainte Mère Eglise mopped up by troopers of the 82nd Airborne, are both secured. To the north, paratroopers of the 82nd AB and riflemen of the 4th ID are pushing toward Montebourg but Lieutenant Colonel Keil's Grenadier Regiment 919 puts out a strong resistance.

Further west, the inundated Merderet valley is a mighty obstacle. The onslaught to cross it starts on June 9th at 10.30 hours on the La Fière causeway with the 325th GIR, 82nd Airborne. Thanks to the new bridgehead established by paratroopers, the 90th Infantry Division gets into the fight and takes Picauville on June 10th.

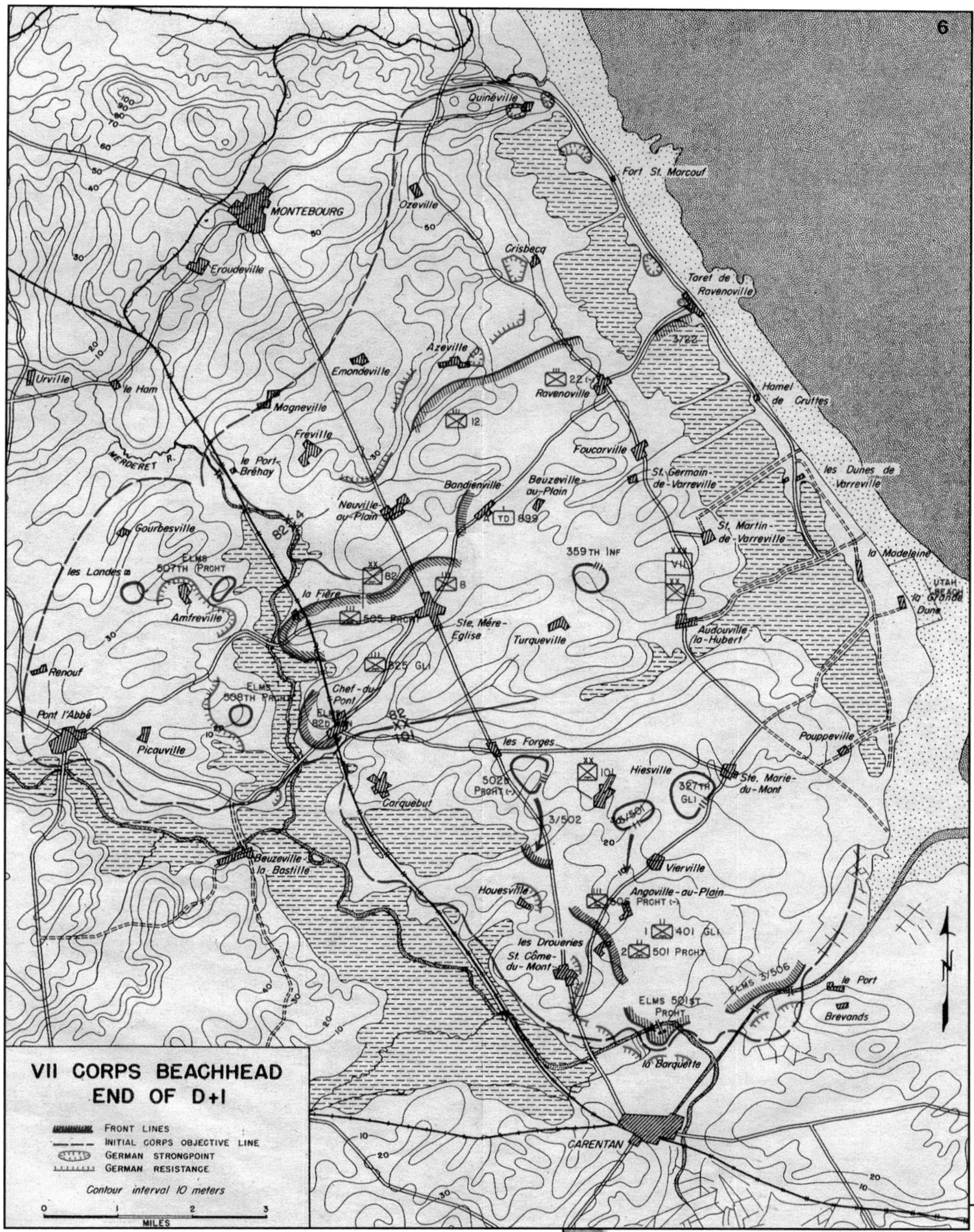

VII CORPS BEACHHEAD
END OF D+I

FRONT LINES
INITIAL CORPS OBJECTIVE LINE
GERMAN STRONGPOINT
GERMAN RESISTANCE

Contour interval 10 meters

0 1 2 3
MILES

6. The American beach head at nighfall on june 7th. The objectives line (dotted line) has not yet been reached. However, the beach head has moved to the north up to Baudienville and Ravenoville thanks to the support of two infantry regiments of the 4th Infantry division, the 12th and 22nd. Neuville au Plain is still uner German threat, and the Azeville and Crisbecq batteries will hold until June 9th. To the west, La Fière and Chef du Pont are in American hands but the river's western bank is still contested by the germans. The Merderet will be crossed in force on June 9th at La Fière. To the south, von der Heydte's parachutists are still hanging to Saint Côme. (US Army map.)

7. A Georgian Lieutenant of Ost-Battaillon 795 made out of Georgian volonteers have put out a strong resistance before giving up in the morning of June 7th. Some of them have been wiped out by the Americans on the 6th at 15.00 at Audouville la Hubert. (US Army.)

8. Now and then, the la Fière Manor, line of departure on the June 9th attack across the causeway. (E.G. /Heimdal.)

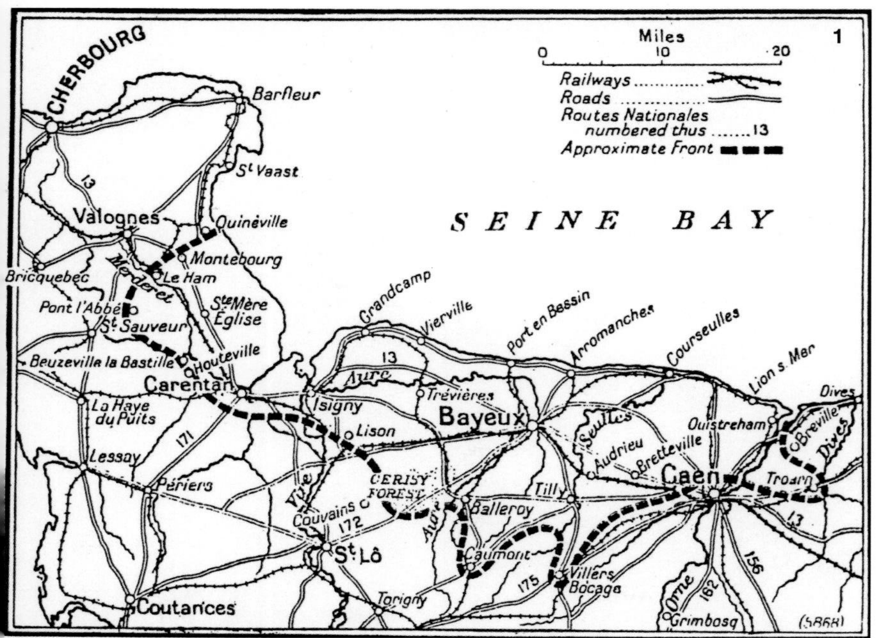

2

3

The airborne bridgehead

Following the British airborne operations successes in the night of June 5th, with the fall of the Orne river bridge and the canal, the Commandos (Lord Lovat and the First Special Service Brigade) and the 6th Airborne Division hold a bridgehead east of the Orne, around Ranville and Amfreville. They are facing to the north east scattered elements of the 716.ID soon reinforced by the 711.ID, and most importantly, to the south and south east, Kampfgruppe Luck (one of the three 21.Panzer-Division tactical groups) commanded by Major Hans von Luck who assembles his infantry regiment, Panzer Grenadier Regiment 125, supported by Major Becker's assault guns (Sturmgeschütz-Abteilung 200), and Panzer IV from the I./22 and artillery. 15.00 hours, June 7th, a German counter attack is under way with Panzer IV of the 4./Panzer-Regiment 22 and the 21.Pz-Div. recon group.This recon unit was commanded by Major Waldow just back from Berlin where he got married. He was soon to die while repelling an attack. On June 13th, a « troop » of 13/18th Royal Hussars is thrown into the bridgehead and Bréville falls at the cost of heavy casualties : 162 KIAs, including 9 officers at the 12th Parachute battalion and the Devons D Company. 550 parachutists jumped into Normandy on June 6th. Only headquarters company and a 5O men company are still accounted for. 77 german bodies (belonging to the 711.ID) wil be recovered inside the destroyed village. But by the end of June 12th reinforcemenst have crossed the Orne : the 152nd Infantry Brigade, 51st Highland Division join up with its advanced elements already in the area.This onslaught will turn into a disaster and its commanding officer will be sacked. This bridgehead will turn into a tough war of attrition for almost a month, until operation Goodwood (see further on). The parachutists and commandos shall remain on line in this sector until august 18th and the german general withdrawal.

1. This period map published in a british newspaper shows the evolution of the front line by June 15th. In the Second British army sector, the Villers-Bocage saliant, an unsuccesful attempt to breackthrough, is clearly visisble, and east of the Orne, the airborne bridgehead.

2. This picture dated June 7th shows Commandos of the 1st Special Service Brigade digging in around their command post shortly after arriving. They shall reamin stuck in this bridgehead for many long weeks. (IWM.)

6

4

7

5

8

3. French commandos of N°4 Commando in Amfreville. From left to right, Commando Paoli, M. Guyard who volunteered on the 8th and is wounded on the 10th (the picture is dated June 9th), Commando Ziwolava, Madam Nicole Michèle, M. Potel, Madam Lefèvre, Commando Wavrault, Commando Gabriel (wounded June 11th) and half hidden, Commando Lanternier. This is the Commando insignia also clearly visible on the soldier's sleeve. (IWM.)

4. The famous Pegasus bridge, a vital supply route within the bridgehead. This picture was taken weeks after D day, with the roadsign just installed on july 12th. This bridge has since been removed and stands next to the Pegasus museum (IWM)

5. On this picture, Major Hans von Luck (center), commanding officer of Kampfgruppe Luck, studies his map acording to informations provided by Leutnant Gerhardt Bandomir, commanding one of von Luck's company, the 3./125. Von Luck carries a 7,65 pistol he will use later on to threaten servants of a flak battery north of Cagny – see further on, Operation Goodwood. (BA.)

6. Hans von Luck (left) and Gerhardt Bandomir back into the bridgehead on June 6th 1990. Both are now deceased. (Coll. G.B.)

7. Kampfgruppe Luck : grenadiers of Panzer-grenadier Regiment 125 surround a I./22 Leutnant wearing the feldgrau assault artillery jacket with the panzer troops head and cross bones, and checking his map. (BA.)

8. 7,5 cm Pak 40 auf Fahrgestell-Panzerkampfwagen 38 (f) of the Sturmgeschütz-Abteilung 200 in operation on Kampfgruppe Luck's sector east of Caen. This is one of the two types of assault guns that equipped this group. It is a very successful odd work by Major Becker who adapted a very effective 75 mm german anti tank gun (7,5 cm Pak 40) to the chassis of an french Hotchkiss tank. The other type is even more effective, using a 105 mm gun. (BA)

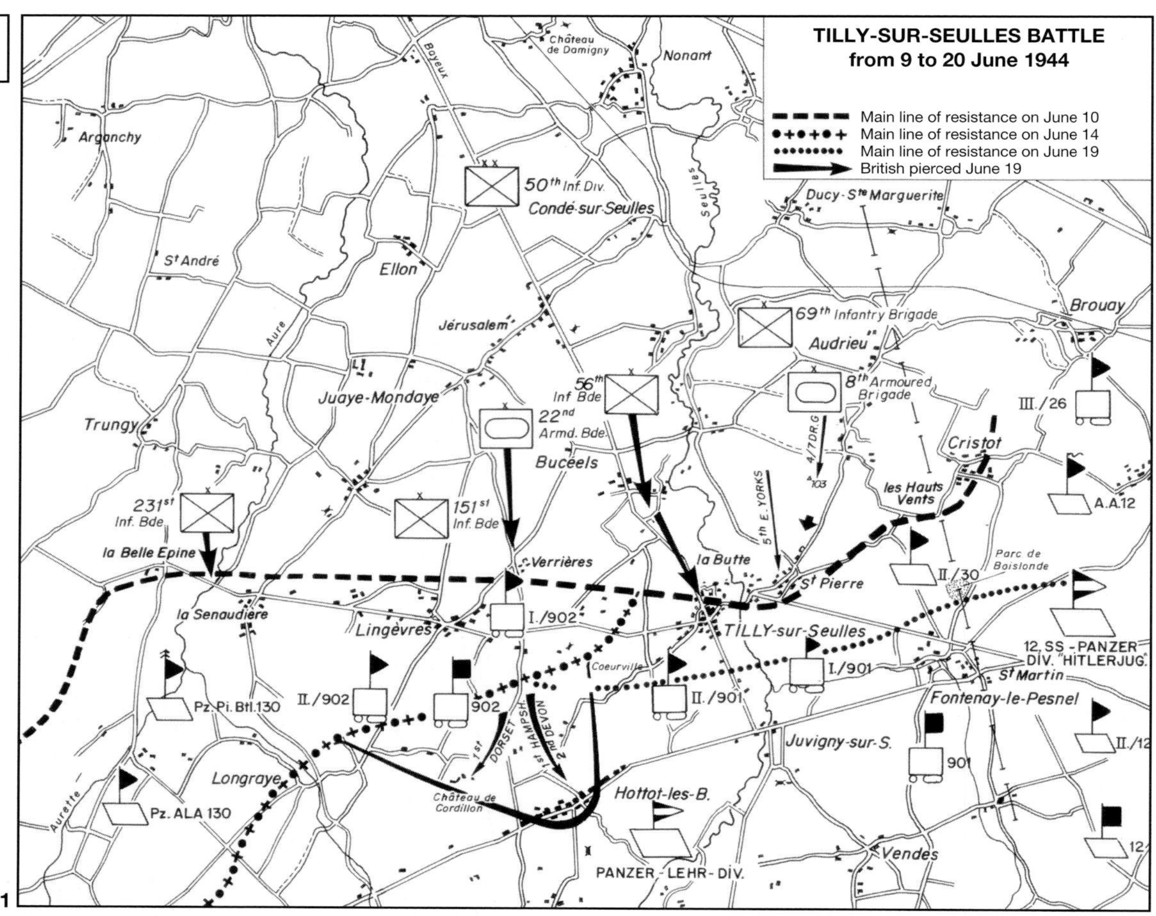

1

2

3

1. Tilly front line from June 9th till June 20th (Heimdal.)

2 and **3.** Sherman tanks from A squadron, 24th Lancers, 8th Armoured Brigade approaching Saint Léger on June 11th. (IWM.)

4. Type H Panzer IV from II./ Panzer-Lehr Regiment 130, one of the two battalions from the PLD Tank Regiment, whose CO Prince von Schoenburg-Waldenburg was KIA on June 11th.The turret protective plates bears his coat of arms, on the side and rear. The numbers on this particular tank from 5th company are painted in an odd way, on each side et on the rear. (Painting by Julio Lopez Caiero).

5. Major Prince von Schoenburg-Waldenburg ; Kommandeur of II./Pz.- Lehr Rgt 130, killed in action on June 11th while trying to take Hill 103. (Coll. H. Ritgen/J.C. Perrigault.)

6. Tombstones of Prince von Schoenburg-Waldenburg, his radio operator, Oberleutnant Hermann, and his aid Karl Füssel, in the cemetery of Parfouru sur Odon. (S. Jacquet)

7. Vickers machine guns of B Company, 2nd Chetshire Regiment on hill 103 on June 13th. (IWM.)

8. Sherman tank Fox, as shown here, is an artillery observer tank. It drives up to the front in the Cristot area where an attack took place on June 16th (IWM.)

Tilly sur Seulles front line

With the arrival south of Bayeux of the Panzer-Lehr-Division, prospects of a quick advance towards Tillys sur Seules soon vanish. Successive local actions lead by the 50th Division all fail. On June 11th, the 2nd Gloster reaches a cross roads at Tilly, but is beaten back by one regiment of the PLD, the 901st Grenadier regiment. Hill 103 between Tilly and Audrieu is harshly contested on June 10th until June 12th. Prince von Schönburg-Waldenburg, commanding officer of II./130, second tank battalion from the PLD dies in his panzer IV while attacking the line between Hill 103 and the hamlet of Saint Pierre on June 11th. This small town is abandonned by the British on June 12th, the « worst day ever » for the 24th Lancers. On the next day, June 13th, with the British still stalled in front of Tilly, the US Vth Corps to the west, facing weak german elements, advances all the way to Caumont L'Eventé, opening a breach in the left flank of the Panzer-Lehr-Division and allowing the 7th Armoured Division to attempt a bold flanking movement around Tilly's western side, to Villers Bocage and up to Caen (See next pages). In the Tilly area, heavy gun fire can be heard from the south, coming from Vil-

lers. On June 13th and 14th, the 1st Hampshire and the 1s Dorset are fighting to secure the Senaudière crossroads. A first attack on Lingèvres is lead by the 6 DLI and the 9 DLI ; tankers of 4th/7th Dragoon Guards claim some success when they knock out 6 Panther tanks within 6 minutes. On June 16th, the British front is strengthened in this area by the 49th West Riding Division, and Cristot falls although defended by elements of the « HJ ». To the west, in the Lingèvres sector, the PLD is under pressure and must fall back to La Senaudière. Further east, the 49th ID is engaged from June 17th until June 21st towards Boislonde castle. In the center, the attack on Tilly is about to begin.

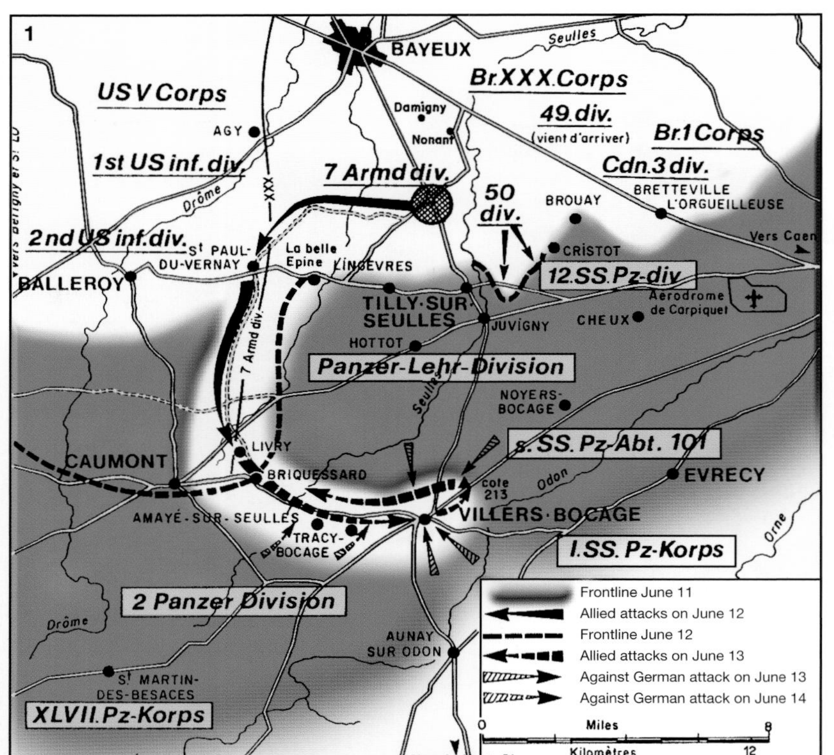

Villers Bocage, (June 12th-13th)

On June 12th, assessing the situation (the US 2nd ID has reached the outskirts of Caumont L'Eventé), General Montgomery decides to launch Operation Perch to outflank the German front and Caen from the south. It becomes 7th Armoured's job. This armoured division distinguished itself in Africa. The 7th AD starts off at 15.00 hours but instead of moving towards Tilly as previously planned, advances in a long column to reach Livry at nightfall (See map) having in the mean time lost the leading tank from the 8th Hussars. The column then heads to the south east and the advance resumes on June 13th at dawn (5.30 hours), towards Villers-Bocage, with A Company 4th CLY (County of London Yeomanry, the «sharpshooters») in the lead. Progress is fast and the lead elements reach Hill 213, above Villers eastern sector, along the Caen heighway, at 8.00 hours ! Rest is ordered, but destiny has its ways.

Two Tiger tanks companies from the schwere SS-Panzer-Abteilung 101 had just reached the area and had settled down for the night : SS-Hauptsturmführer Ralph Moebius'1st company, to the north of the heighway, and tank ace SS-Obersturmführer (Lieutenant) Michael Wittman's 2nd company on the southern shoulder. They had been alerted by the Panzer-Lehr-Division on the incoming attack, with all the previous skirmishes, but knew nothing of where it came from. All of a sudden, they found themselves in the immediate proximity of the advancing armored column. They immediately launch a counterattack. Wittman storms down the Villers heighway, wrecking havoc among the stalled armored column. A dozen tanks and a great deal of vehicles are destroyed. The german propaganda will exploit this feat of arm. The onslaught is stopped downtown Villers by British defenders. But the attack of the 7th Armoured is broken, and it must pull out of Villers at nightfall. The front shall remained in this stalled position west of Villers until early august, when all german forces will pull back after the american breakthrough.

7th Armoured Division

I.SS-Pz.-Korps

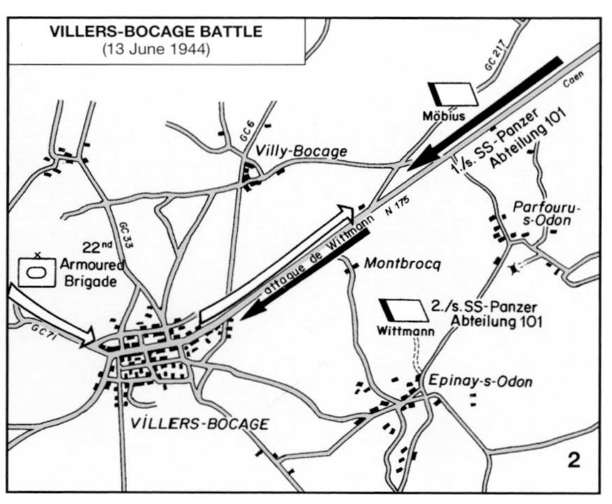

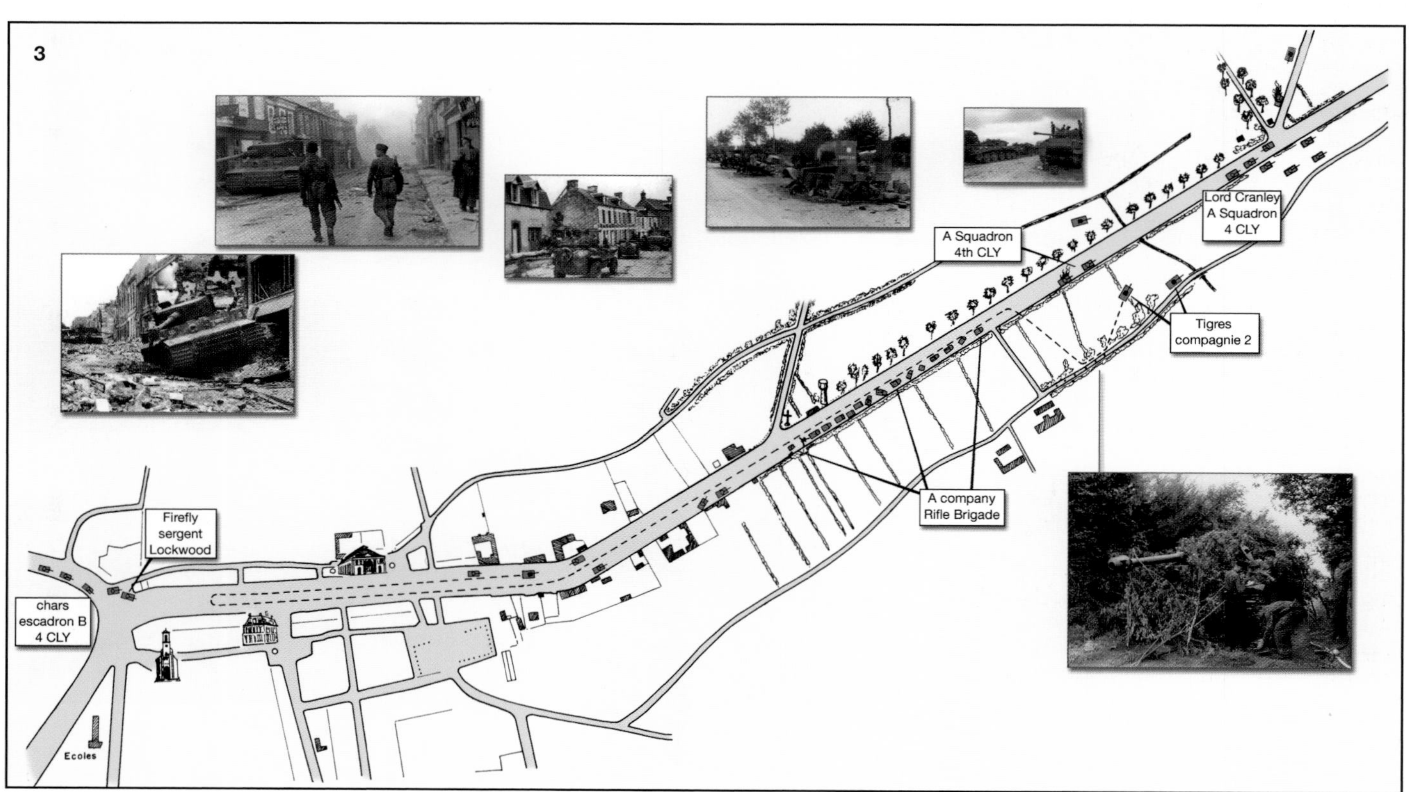

1. This map points out the flanking movements achieved by the 7th Armoured Division on the western end of the British front, from the 50th ID rear and using the american breakthrough at Caumont L'Eventé (See front line on June 12th). This division moves up to Livry and then to Villers-Bocage on June 13th thus outflanking the German front. (Heimdal map)

2. This map shows the advance of the 22nd Armoured Brigade on June 13th through Villers-Bocage on to Hill 213, followed by the counter attack lead by two Tiger tanks companies from the s. SS-Pz-Abt. 101, Möbius 1st to the north of the road and Wittman's 2nd, to the south and all the way within Villers-Bocage. (Heimdal)

3. Detailed map showing destroyed British armoured vehicles (A/Rifle Brigade, A/4 CLY) from the town's limit to Hill 213, and the Tigers attack towards the city Hall. (Heimdal.)

4. This picture taken from the water reservoir (See map N°3) shows some of the wrecked vehicles (Half tracks, Loyd-Carriers, Bren Carriers) belonging to the Rifle Brigade. (BA)

5. Same area, close to the crossroads, with Tilly to the left. Colour photograph published by Signal and showing the tree lined road to Caen, with Hill 213 at the top. In the foreground lies a 57 mm anti tank gun set up close to the calvary. (Coll. Heimdal)

6 and **7.** Further down the road, in the curve at the edge of Villers-Bocage, three tanks have been knocked out of action, two Cromwells (one is clearly visible on the right) and one Panzer IV from the II./Panzer-Lehr-Regiment 130 sent to counter attack (bearing Prince von Schoenburg-Waldenburg's coat of arms – the Prince had been killed two days earlier). This is one of the few places where houses remained intact, making the location easy to identify in spite of some modern renovations. (BA and Heimdal.)

8. This particular picture shows the wreckage of the three panzers that lead the counter attack, one Tiger from 1st Company, another Tiger and a Panzer IV from the PLD. (BA.)

Michael Wittmann

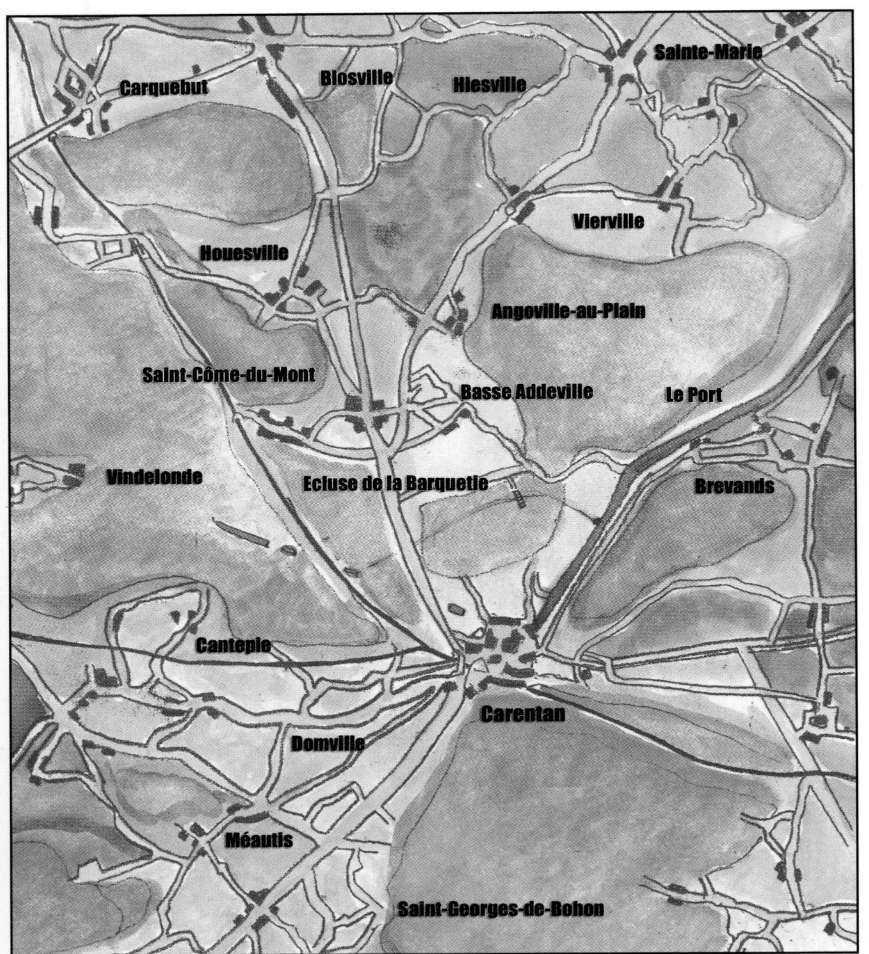

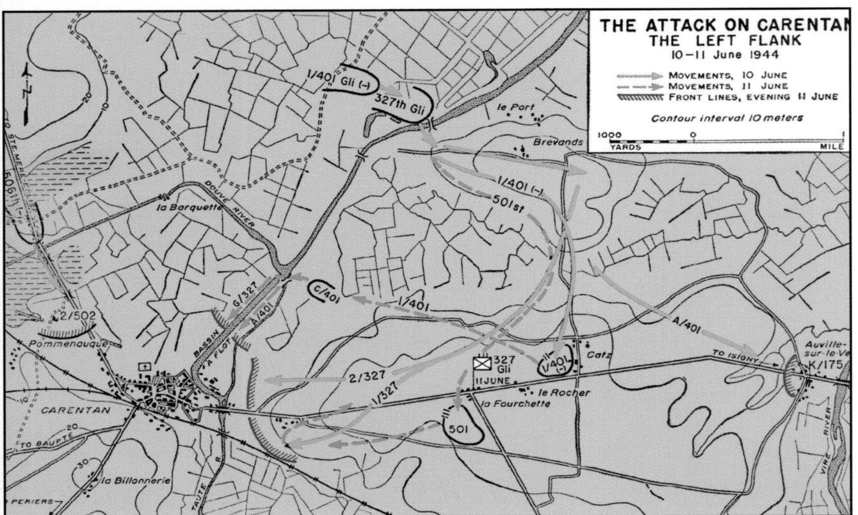

1. Map showing the expand of the inundated areas around Carentan in June 1944. One can see Saint Côme du Mont to the North, the La Barquette Locks and Sainte Marie du Mont. Carentan is shaped like an isthmus and is a strategic road junctions in the middle of marshes area (Map by EG/Heimdal)

2. The June 10th and 11th assault on Carentan ; a large outflanking movement lead by the 327th GIR (with its attached 1/401st battalion) crossing the Douve river on the northern edge of town. One company (A/401st) links up with the 29th Division (K/175th) at Auville sur le Vey. The two beach heads are at long last connected. The final push is accomplished by the 502nd PIR from the west, G/327th and A/401st from the north while the two remaining battalions of the 327th GIR slip through from the east. The grey portions show the ground gained by june 11th in the evening. (Heimdal with US Army).

3. Carentan, looking towards the bridges, close to the railroad tracks (Désiré Ingouf house to the left). US soldiers riding on an abandonned german FJ Kübelwagen. Licence plate shows WL for Luftwaffe. (US Army)

The final fight for Carentan

The attack resumes at dawn on June 10th on the bridges leading to Carentan with american paratroopers of the 502nd PIR, 101st Airborne. They are stopped cold by Major von der Heydte's german parachutists. The Major has his FJR6 disposed in a half circle around Carentan. In the early hours of June 11th, Lieutenant Colonel Robert Cole's 3/502 attacks in the direction of the « cabbage patch ». Cole will be awarded the Medal of Honor for this action. Elsewhere, other elements of the 101st Airborne (327th GIR and 1/401st GIR) attack Carentan from the north and east. Low on ammunition and threatened to be surrounded, Major von der Heydte orders an withdrawal at 16.00 hours and moves his parchutists to prepared defensive positions to the south of town. The withdrawal is effective during the night of June 11th. There's no decisive battle for Carentan. Elements of the 101st Airborne enter Carentan at dawn from the west, north and east, and find the city evacuated. The German parachutists fought in Carentan a stubborn battle until they ran out of ammunition. They are from then on called the « Lions of Carentan ».

As von der Heydte's Fallschirmjaeger-Regiment 6 settles into a new main line of resistance, a german full division comes to the rescue ; the 17.SS-Panzergrenadier-Division « Götz von Berlichingen ». It launches an attack on June 13th from the Périer-Carentan road. It is supported by assault guns (1. and 2./SS- Pz.-Abt. 17) and shakes the american defenders. The Germans are on the immediate outskirts of Carentan, in the railroad station area. The 2nd US Armored division comes to the rescue of the exausted paratroopers. Jumping off from the Omaha beach head, tanks of the CCA2 and 105 mm « Priests » assault guns from the 14th Field Artillery Battalion save the day. The German assault is repulsed. Carentan becomes an essential communication hub between the two american beach heads. But the front in this area from Carentan and Sainteny will be for many weeks hotly contested by the « Götz » and the surviving Fallschirmjaeger.

4. Other US paratroopers have « liberated » a german tracked motorcycle called Kettenkrad. (Coll. Heimdal)

5. Picture taken on June 18th in Carentan, after the german counter attack. It shows an american 105 mm self propelled gun from the 14th Field Artillery Battalion (2nd Armored Division) driving back from the front and moving across the railroad tracks (The Désiré Ingouf house is to the right, unseen on this picture). (US Army)

6. Nowadays, the railroad crossing no longer exists (E.G. Heimdal)

7. South of Carentan, along the Périers road, americans have set up an anti tank gun ahead of a knocked out StuG III from the SS-Pz. Abt. 17. (US Army.)

8. Same place nowadays ; this all important crossroads leading west on the left hand side to Baupte (E.G. Heimdal)

9. The june 18th meeting between SS-Brigadeführer Ostendorf (left), Kommandeur of the « Götz » and Major von der Heydte.

10. The 17.SS-Pz. Gren. Div ; coat of arms, the steel glove of the 16th Century Knight Götz von Berlichingen.

9th Infantry Division

Westward : Saint Sauveur le Vicomte

West of the Merderet, the 90th Infantry Division, after liberating Picauville on the 10th of June, lacking steam and experience comes to a halt. Progress is slow on June 12th and 13th. The 357th Infantry regiment loses 150 men each day ! Facing stubborn german resistance, the Americans heavily bomb Pont L'Abbé on June 12th around 5.00 pm. They walk into a ruined and devastated town in the night of June 12th. The failure of this offensive cost Major General Mc Kelvie his 90th division. He is relieved and replaced by Major General Eugen M Landrum. Furthermore, Major General Collins, boss of VII Corps brings up on the line an already exausted 82nd Airborne Division in order to reinforce the « green » 90th ID.

In the early hours of June 14th, 82nd Airborne troopers advance west of Pont l'Abbé and reach the Bonneville sector. On June 15th, the 82nd Airborne makes further progress on each side of the road to Saint Sauveur le Vicomte. The attack to take that town starts on June 16th at dawn. The Americans face the town dominated by a medieval castle. They hold the eastern side of the Douve river. Once the river crossed, they enter Saint Sauveur at nightfall. Further north, on the right flank, the 9th Infantry Division has broken through the german lines in the Orglandes sector and pushes forward to Sainte Colombe and

1. Starting June 14th, with the 90 th ID on its right flank, the 82nd Airborne Division moves west, using Pont l'Abbé (picture) as a line of departure. The 90th ID had been badly mauled trying to take this little town in ruins. (Coll. Heimdal)

2. Lieutenant Kelso C. Horne (First platoon, I Company, 508th PIR) stages a posture for the camera with his M-1 Garand. After 10 days of fierce fighting, the US paratroopers still wage an incredibly agressive war to the Germans. (NA/Heimdal.)

3. This aerial photo taken looking east, shows Saint Sauveur le Vicomte, in ruins, with its medieval donjon sticking out to the left. In the background runs the Pont l'Abbé road and the Douve river. (NA/Heimdal.)

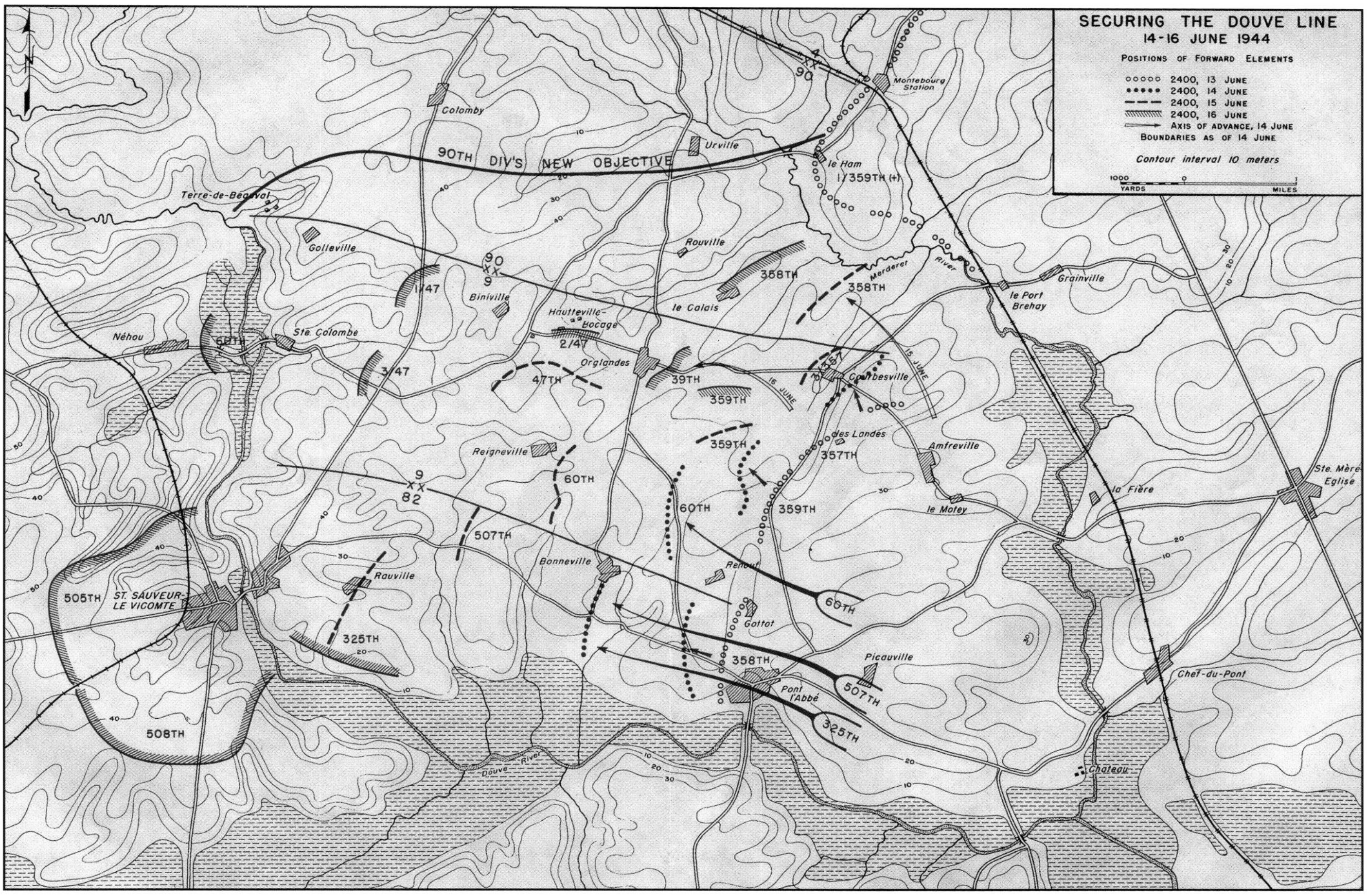

SECURING THE DOUVE LINE
14-16 JUNE 1944

POSITIONS OF FORWARD ELEMENTS
2400, 13 JUNE
2400, 14 JUNE
2400, 15 JUNE
2400, 16 JUNE
AXIS OF ADVANCE, 14 JUNE
BOUNDARIES AS OF 14 JUNE

Contour interval 10 meters

4

4. Map showing the advance of three american divisions towards their next obstacle, the Douve river, between june 14th and 16th. Picauville fell on the 10th, Pont L'Abbé on the 13th and Saint-Sauveur-le-Vicomte on the 16th, as the Germans pulled back. (US Army)

Néhou aiming for the sea shore and the split of the Cotentin peninsula.

5. Inside Saint Sauveur, a paratrooper moves up amidst burning houses, Bottin-Desylles street, facing towards the railroad station still in german hands. (NA/Heimdal)

6 and 7. On this famous photo, Lieutenant Colonel Benjamin Vandervoort still on crutches stands among the rubbles of Saint Sauveur le Vicomte. The road sign indicating La Haye du Puits is clearly visible. It will take the Americans another month to seize that town. Today, the entire road intersection has been rebuilt. (NA et E.G./Heimdal.)

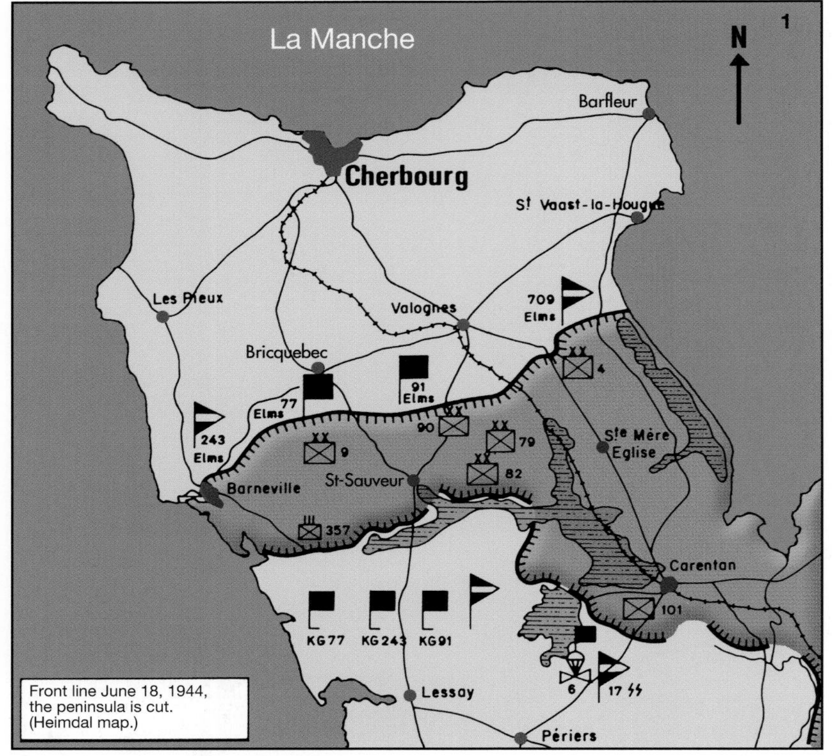

Front line June 18, 1944, the peninsula is cut. (Heimdal map.)

Objective, Cherbourg

The advance to Montebourg being rough, the western offensive takes on a new start as early as June 17th with the sole 9th Infantry Division aiming for the western shore of the Cotentin. On the 18th at dawn, K Company, 3/60th, after an all night march, seteles down on open ground dominating Barneville. The sea is at reach, and the peninsula severed.

The Germans counter attack on each side to avoid encirclement. But the breakthrough has also split in half many divisions holding the area, especially the 77. ID just arrived from Brittany. Some of its elements try to make good their escape towards the south following the road from Bricquebec to Barneville. The 60th Field Artilleru Battalion open up with its batteries and inflict heavy casualkties to the fleeing germans. General Hellmich (243. ID) is killed on the 17th, General Stegmann (77.ID) on the 18th. The elements who made it through will then fight on as Kampfgruppen, tactical groups that wil fight firther south, such as KG Bacherer (bearing its CO's name and constituted with elements from the 77.ID), KG 243. ID, KG 91. ID. On that day, the trap closes down on the remnants of these divisions and on the 709.ID surrounded inside a large pocket still commanded by General von Schlieben, Kommandeur of the 709 ID.

Collins, Commanding officer of the VII Corps, puts 4 divisions on the line for the final push westward : 9th ID (Major General Eddy), 90th ID (Major General Landrum), 79th ID (Major General Wyche), 4th ID (Major General Barton). At the last moment, the failing 90th ID is not included. Faced with these new developments, the german leaders orders a general retreat inside festung Cherbourg. Defensive positions have been prepared in a semi circle, anchored on two defensive strongpoints, Osteck and Westeck. Cherbourg, a large military harbor wide open to the sea appears difficult to protect. On June 19th at midday, the order to withdraw is passed along the german lines. The Americans, unaware of the situation, move out cautiosly, fearing some kind of a trick. The 9th ID reaches the wester part of the Festung on the 20th, cutting off the german strongpoits in la Hague. Von Schlieben's defensive elements are alerted, ready to fight, but without much illusions.

1. This map shows the new front line on June 18th. The 9th Infantry Division has split the Cotentin peninsula taking Barneville. Elements from four German divisions are now isolated, cut off in the north (243rd, 77th, 91st and 709th). Some units from these divisions have successfully retreated to the south and avoid encirclement. Four divisions, then three (9th, 79th and 4th from the west to the east) are making progress towards Cherbourg, facing Germans retreating to their Festung (Heimdal).

2. Near Bricquebec, medics from the 39th IR of the 9th ID provide a wounded german soldier with a glass of wine. He probably belongs to the 77th ID that fell under american fire on the road from Barneville to Bricquebec. Worth noticing on one of the medics helmet a typical 39th IR stencil marking : AAAO, meaning Anytime Anything Anywhere bar nothing. (NA)

3. Helmet bearing this marking. (Private coll.)

4. and **5.** After the german retreat, american soldiers from the 4th ID finally walk into Montebourg, clear of Germans and in ruins on June 20th. Then and now picture. (NA and E.G./Heimdal.)

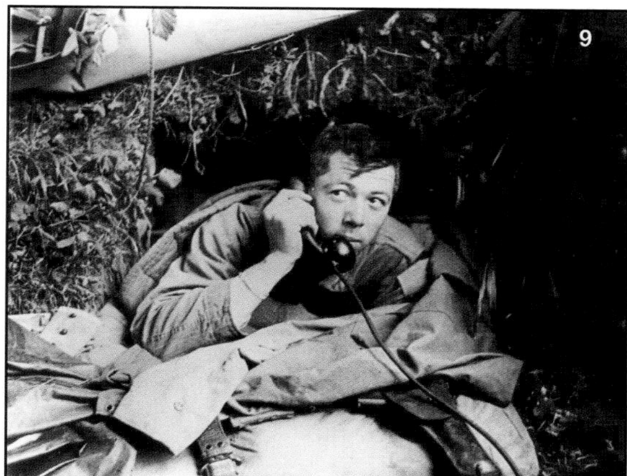

6 and **7.** This picture was shot south of Montebourg next to the old front line that used to stand there until the morning of June 19th when KG Keil (III./919) pulled out. These positions looked straight down into town. (NA et E.G./Heimdal.)

8. Valognes. Outstanding color picture taken in 1944 and showing the ruined Saint Malo church in the heart of what used to be called a « Norman Versailles », now crushed to rubbles by the bombings. (NA)

9. Lieutenant George Mutter (US Soldier of german descend) directing artillery fire on the external defenses of Cherbourg. (NA./Heimdal.)

10. Two riflemen from the 39th IR, 9th ID lobbing grenades over a wall. In this close quartered battlefield, hand to hand fighting occurs frequently. One helmet shows distinctively the AAAO marking. (Coll. Heimdal.)

The storm (June 19th-22nd)

A violent storm came with the summer solstice from June 19th til 22nd. Strong winds from the north east hit the coast for over 72 hours. In the early hours of june 19th, a north east wind swept the Channel and along the southern coasts of England all embarkations sought safety inside the harbors. But off the Normandy beaches, all kinds of boats in different types or sizes were washed up to the shore. Mulberry artificial harbors, especially Mulberry A in the american sector began to desintegrate. Huge Phoenix caissons were knocked out of place and waves rushed madly into the Mulberry harbor. The resisting Blockships alone avoided total disaster. Mulberry A, off Saint Laurent sur Mer (Omaha Beach) was the most exposed harbor. The floating roads were destroyed and some Phoenix caissons broke in half, hit by loose ships. All along the beach laid wreckages of Landing ships (over 600 of them will be lost) and the shore was littered with all kind of debris. All unloading missions had to be cancelled. On June 18th, 24 412 tons of supply and ammunitions were delivered into Normandy, a peak in the supply mission. But in the evening of June 20 only 4 560 tons had been unloaded, mostly on Mulberry B in Arromanches.

1. Mulberry B (Arromanches) and its floating roads with offshore the breakwater made out of Phoenix caissons. This artificial harbor is a true technical wonder that allowed the quick delivery of large amounts of supplies to the ground forces. (IWM)

2 and **3.** After the storm. Here are elements of the floating roads washed up to the shore, sunken boats and a general desolate view of Arromanches whose Mulberry harbor will eventually be repaired using parts of Mulberry A. (IWM.)

4. Mulberry A (Omaha) has suffered heavily and will not be fixed. (NA.)

2

1 While the VIII Corps onslaught reaches the bottom of Hill 112, the Panzer-Lehr-Division and the 12.SS-Pz.Div. whose main line of resistance has jus collapsed, get reinforcements ; one regiment of 1.SS-Pz.-Div. LAH in the east, KG Weidinger to the west. The II.SS-Panzer-Korps comes to the rescue bringing the 9. SS-Pz.Div « Hohenstaufen » and the 10.SS-Pz.div « Frundsberg ». (HF map/Heimdal.)

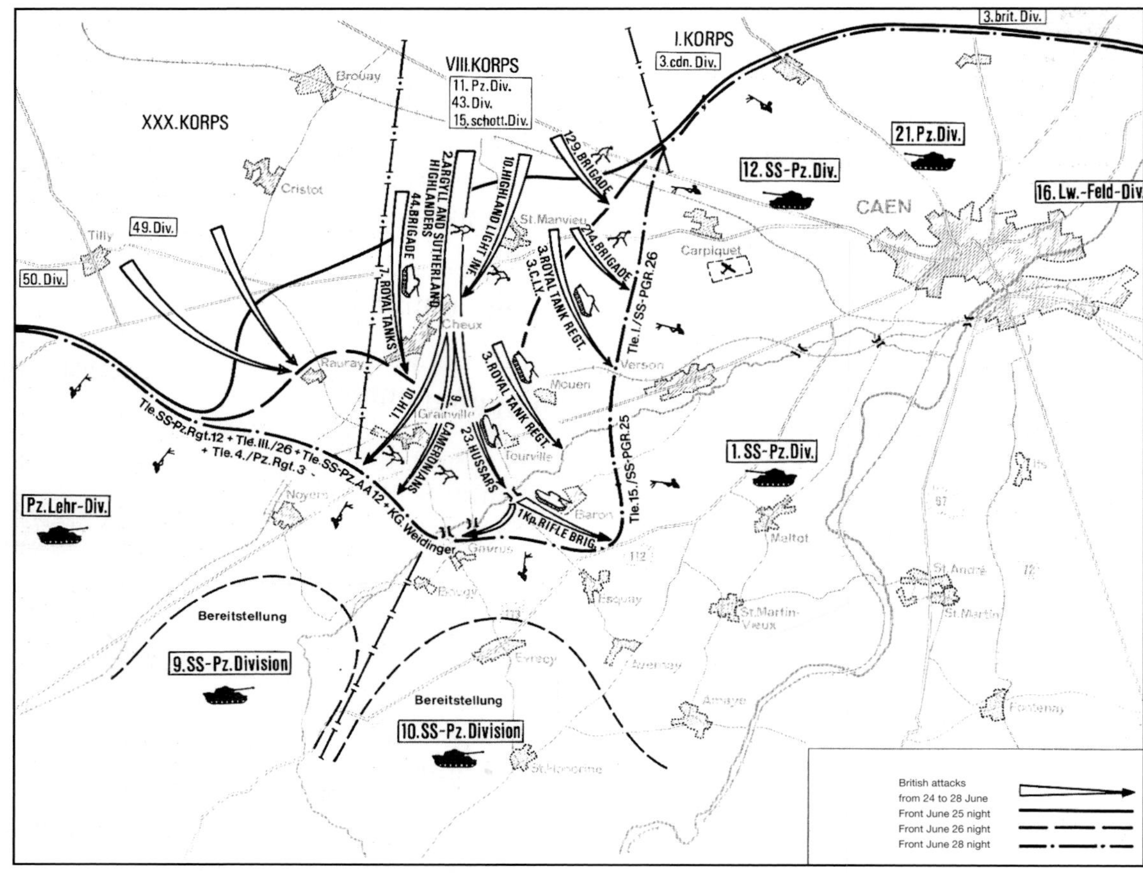

1

15th Scottish Division

11th Armoured Division

43rd Wessex Division

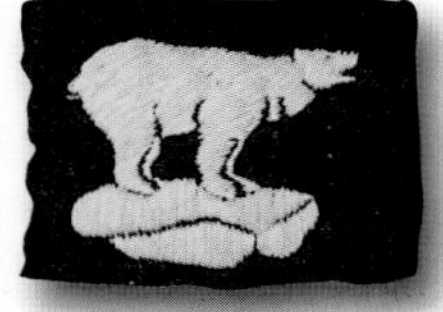

49th West Riding Division

The Odon battle (June 25th-30th)

On a Sunday June 25th, General Montgomery launches Operation Martlet east of Tilly sur Seules. A week earlier, on June 18th, he issued a new order : « We must take Caen and Cherbourg now as the first stage in the developpment of our plans. » The storm slowed down these plans. Montgomery engages one new Corps, VIII Corps (15th Scottish Division, 43rd Essex Division and the 11th Armoured Division). But before committing these three divisions in battle, the 49th West Riding Division (XXX Corps committed in the Tilly sector) must first clear the right flank in order to ease the way for VIII Corps. Fontenay le Pesnel must fall, but the going gets tough against elements of the PLD (I./901) in the west and III./26 (HJ). Results are unsatisfactory for the « Polar bears » of the 49th Division ; most of the objectives have not been reached, Rauray in particular, supposed to cover the VIII Corps flank.

On June 26th the main offensive (Operation Epsom) starts with VIII Corps ; The Odon valley must be crossed in order to reach Hill 112 and the high grounds above the area, then rush through the Orne valley and take the Falaise road outflanking Caen from the south. VIII Corps outpowers the german defenders, 60 000 men vs less than 2 000 ! ; facing him are only two battalions of the Hitlerjugend Division (an Engineer battalion and the I./206). The german front collapses after an intense artillery barrage, with only a few pockets of resistance by HJ Grenadiers whose stubborness astonishes the British. Although overrun, the survivors keep on shooting at the assaliants who in turn overestimate the german resistance and stop their avance. Some panzers of the HJ division, mostly from 5./12 and 8./12, Ostuf. Siegel commanding, stop cold the British offensive south of Cheux with almost no defenders left behind those few german strongpoints. Hill 112 could have been taken along the way, as only a couple of hundreds of elite soldiers brought the entire assault to a halt.

Tuesday June 27th, this respite buys the Germans time to reorganize and receive reinforcements : the II.SS-Panzer-Korps, with the 9.SS-Pz.Div « Hohenstaufen » and the 10. SS-Pz. Div. « Frundsberg » on their way to counter attack east of Balleroy is rushed to the area. This very same day, Rauray finally falls and the Odon valley is crossed. But on the 28th, an over careful advance allows a few panzers belonging to the Hitlerjugend to withdraw on Hill 112 ; this major stategic strongpoint, still unoccupied in the morning, is now firmly held in spite of the 29th Armoure Brigade tanks. Elsewhere, elements of the Leibstandarte counter attack in the east out of Verson and KG Weidinger from the west in the Rauray sector. On Thursday June 29th, elements of the Leibstandarte are repulsed but the Hohenstaufen gets into the fight (Rauray and Grainville sur Odon sector) as well as the Frundsberg on hill 113. These attacks by those two powerful divisions are crushed by naval artillery guns firing from the sea. These attacks falter and on friday June 30th, further fightings in the Hill 112 area seals each side hopes for a decisive outcome. The Odon river has been crossed but the « scottish corridor » has turned into a dead

2 and **3.** Fontenay le Pesnel, June 25th. This dramatic photo was taken on the Tilly sur Seules road leading to Caen, on the northern edge of village looking east. The german Pak 40 gun in the foreground was pointing at the road running from Hauts Vents and the one coming from Cristot. This is where the XXX british Corps attack came from. Further up is the wreckage of a Sherman tank on the left and a knocked out Panther to the right. The body of a dead Waffen-SS (HJ) lays near the gun. On the « now and then » picture the damaged houses have disappeared, levelled after the war and rebuilt further behind. Only the farm building in the back helps to identify this place. (IWM and G.B.)

3

6

5

8

2

4

7

end facing Hill 112. Against all odds, the battle for the Odon is lost for Montgomery, due to over carefullness when tanks of the 11th Armoured division could have poured into a huge gap.

4 and **5.** Crossroads south east of Fontenay le Pesnel on June 25th. The Panther tank « 219 » of the « HitlerJugend » returns from the northern intersection where it engaged the 11th Royal Scots Fusiliers (Coll. Heimdal and G.B.)

6. Rifleman of B Company, 6 Royal Scots Fusiliers, 15th Scottish Division on the morning of June 26th before the attack on Saint Manvieu. This company will suffer 50% casualties after taking this village, because of determined resistance by grenadiers of the Hitlerjugend. (IWM. Doc. Heimdal.)

7. Scottish riflemen of 12 Platoon, B Company, 6 Royal Scots Fusiliers in Saint Manvieu : faces look tense after suffering heavy casualties. (IWM.)

8. Rauray, June 28th. Two riflemen of the 70th Brigade take a close look at a Tiger tank Type E, 3./s.SS-Pz.Abt. 101 knocked out during a counter, attack. (IWM.)

June 22d-30th

1. June 23rd, all out advance towards the Festung. (Heimdal.)

2. American artillery plays a decisive part in the fall of the Festung. On June 25th, south of Cherbourg, close to the Pierre Butée (9th ID area), artillery forward observers for three divisions are zeroing in their respective guns on German positions in Cherbourg (NA./Heimdal.)

3. The ultimate fights for the Festung are particularly harsh claiming many casualties. This american dogface tells the story after digging his foxhole on the hard Norman soil. (Coll. Heimdal.)

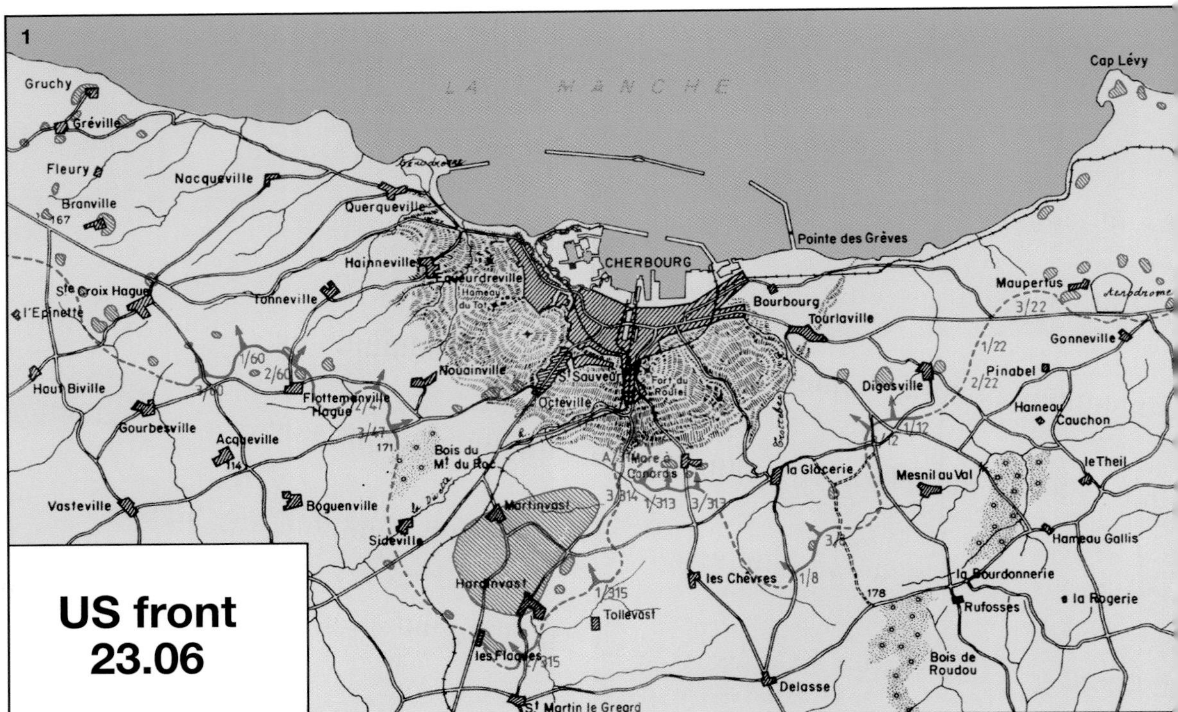

4. On June 24th, the 79th ID crushes the last German strongpoints along the road to Cherbourg and the Fort du Roulle, breaking through Les Chèvres and La mare au Canard. GIs clearing up the bunkers. (Heimdal.)

5. An imposing figure, General von Schlieben and Admiral Hennecke surrender on June 26th at 14.00 hours. They are being lead to the château de Servigny to sign the unconditional surrender with Lt Gen. J. Lawton Collins. (Coll. Heimdal.)

6. Rare color picture shot on Cherbourg streets after the German surrender. (US Army)

7 and **8.** June 26 1944 ; US tanks moving through Toularville, east of Cherbourg. Photo shot on Val de Saire street. Then and now. (NA et E.G./Heimdal.)

Cherbourg, the final battle

In the night of June 21st, Lt Gen Collins sent General von Schlieben an ultimatum, emphasizing the desperate situation german forces were in, and asking for the surrender of Cherbourg . This ultimatum would expire in June 22nd at 19.00 hours. The order to attack came at 09.40 hours. In the west, the 9th ID advances slowly against the german strongpoints. In the center, the 79th ID must break through three successive defensive lines but only succeeds to overrun the first one. In the east, the 4th ID faces KG Rohrbach but its two regiments fail, sustaining heavy

5

4

6

casualties. The June 23rd objectives remain the same ; the 4th ID once again stalls, while the 79th ID gets closer to Fort du Roule and the 9th ID gains some ground towards La Hague. The final onslaught is staged for the 24th of June ; the 4th ID gets around Cherbourg eastern side. By nightfall, the 3 american divisions have a hold on Cherbourg. The 7th ID now looks down on the Roule, the 9th ID is closing on the german underground headquarters in Octeville. The city of Cherbourg is surrounded by high grounds now under american control. The bitter end is nearing for the Germans.

On June 25th, the Fort du Roule that looks upon the City is finally taken thanks to a bold move by Lieutenant Carlos C Ogden and Corporal John D Kelly. For many days, the Germans had been mercilessly pounded par Allied bombers and artillery, and GIs began to pour between the defensive lines and strongpoints. Their line of departure is on the eastern bank of the Divette. Von Schlieben's headquarters is in a desperate situation. On a Monday June 26th, the Fort du Roule is overwhelmed, and more than 300 german soldiers surrender in the evening. At 14.00 hours, von Schlieben still inside his headquarters surrender. The city is liberated, but a Fregattenkapitän Witt keeps on fighting in the fortified arsenal, and inside the bunkers built over the harbors dikes. On June 27th, Cherbourg is taken but some points still resist. Witt from inside the dikes, and Keil surrounded in the La Hague area with over 6 000 men keeps up the fight. Osteck surrenders at 20.00 hours. Witt follows the next day, and Keil finally gives himself up on the 30th. By july 1st, it's all over. The americans herd 39 000 prisonners of war and the Cotentin battle is the Allieds first significant victory ; they hold a large beach head with a deep sea harbor. The Germans have destroyed most of the port installations before the surrender. The liberation of Cherbourg initially and according to plans was to take place at D+15. It happened at D+21. It will take the american engineers only 3 weeks to render the harbor fully operational.

8

7

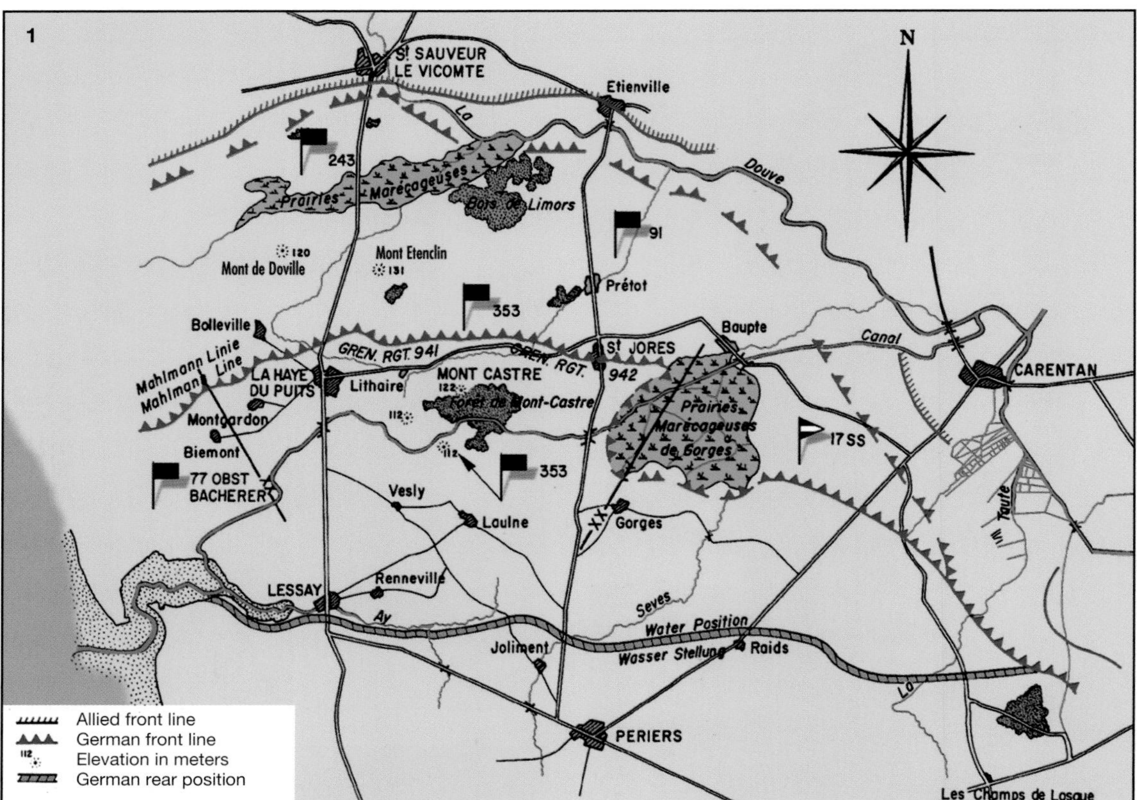

1. Shown here are the lines of defenses set up by the Germans in front of La Haye du Puits : a full line of outposts, the Mahlmann Line (Main Line of Resistance anchored on the Montgardon heights and the Mont Castre), the water line (last resort). (Heimdal map according to US documents on the 353rd ID)

2. Evolution of the front line in the La Haye du Puits sector from July 3rd until 7th, on the northern edge of town. The two first German Lines appear but not the third one. (US Army).

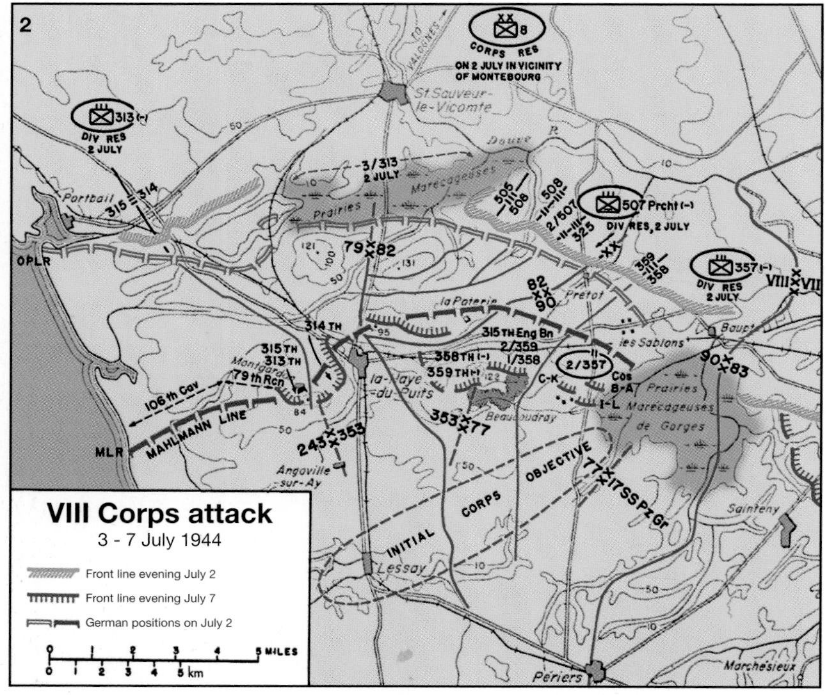

3. VIII. Corps cloth insignia.

4. July 6th, soldiers of the 90th Infantry Division move through Gorges coming from the south of the front line. (DAVA/Heimdal.)

5. Next day, July 7th, near saint Jores, GIs of the same outfit (Division shoulder insignia visible on the soldier standing to the left) move out along hedgerows under cover of a C Company Sherman tank. Road has been cleared of mines. (DAVA/Heimdal.)

6. Three kilometers south of Saint Jores, men of the 90th Infantry division sort out heavy mortar shells. Picture shot on July 7th. (DAVA/ Heimdal.)

7. To cross the Sensurière marshes, B Company, 16th Engineer Combat Battalion built up a Bailey bridge and a boat bridge from Pont L'Abbé in support of the offensive to the Mont Castre. (DAVA/Heimdal.)

First battle of La Haye du Puits (July 3rd-7th)

Once the battle for Cherbourg over, the american chiefs of staff spread out the available forces in 4 army corps all heading south ; V Corps that landed in Omaha and engaged for a month on the western side of the Calvados, XIX Corps, freshly arrived north of Saint Lô, VII Corps (Collins) south of Carentan, VIII Corps north of La Haye du Puits. New divisions reinforce the strategic set up. In front of VIII corps sector, the retreating german units have established a new front based on a three defensive lines: a first line made out of outposts around the la Sensurière marshes, the main line of resistance (Mahlmann line) anchored on the Montgardon heights to the west and the Mont Castre. But the Americans have missed the opportunity for a quick victory. While marching on to Cherbourg, they forgot about this precise sector, leaving the Germans with plenty of time to consolidate. Their moral, once at the lowest, is up again (according to US Intelligence). The battle for La Haye du Puits is bound to last.

VIII Corps (Major General Troy Middleton commanding) moves up to the offensive on July 2nd using, from west to east, the 79th ID, the 82nd Airborne Division and the 90th ID. The assault starts on july 3rd under thin rain that forbids the use of aerial cover. The attack goes according to plans on the western flank but stalls at the bottom of Mont Castre. On the 4th, the 79th ID takes Mont de Doville only lightly defended by a small outpost. It is however soon pinned down by german artillery when approaching La Haye du Puits. It is tough going for the 82nd AB paratroopers and the riflemen of the 90th ID, soaked by rain, at the bottom of Mont Castre also known as « Mount Terrible ». The Germans also suffer terrible losses and have no reserve to make out for them. The 15th Fallschirmjaeger Regiment is on the way. On July 5th the german defense solely relies on the 353rd ID and its great observation point at the top of Mont castre. The weather

8. In Prétot, these GIs leave the front line without any regrets... (DAVA.)

improves and air cover is expected. However, VIII Corps is not making great progresses in spite of the 70th ID attack on Montgardon, quickly repulsed. The Germans have pulled back to their main line of resistance. On July 6th, the 82nd Airborne Division, exausted, is relieved by the 8th ID and return to England. To the west, the 79th ID finally reaches and takes the Mongardon heights. Tough times for the 90th ID climbing up the Mont Castre ; two of its companies are surrounded in Beaucoudray. One of them surrender on the 7th, while the other one pulls back. And Colonel Gröschke's Fallschirmjaeger Regiment 15 arrives in the vicinity of Mont Castre. Another reinforcement is expected, the 2.SS-Panzer-Division « Das Reich » whose forward elements have arrived on the 5th.

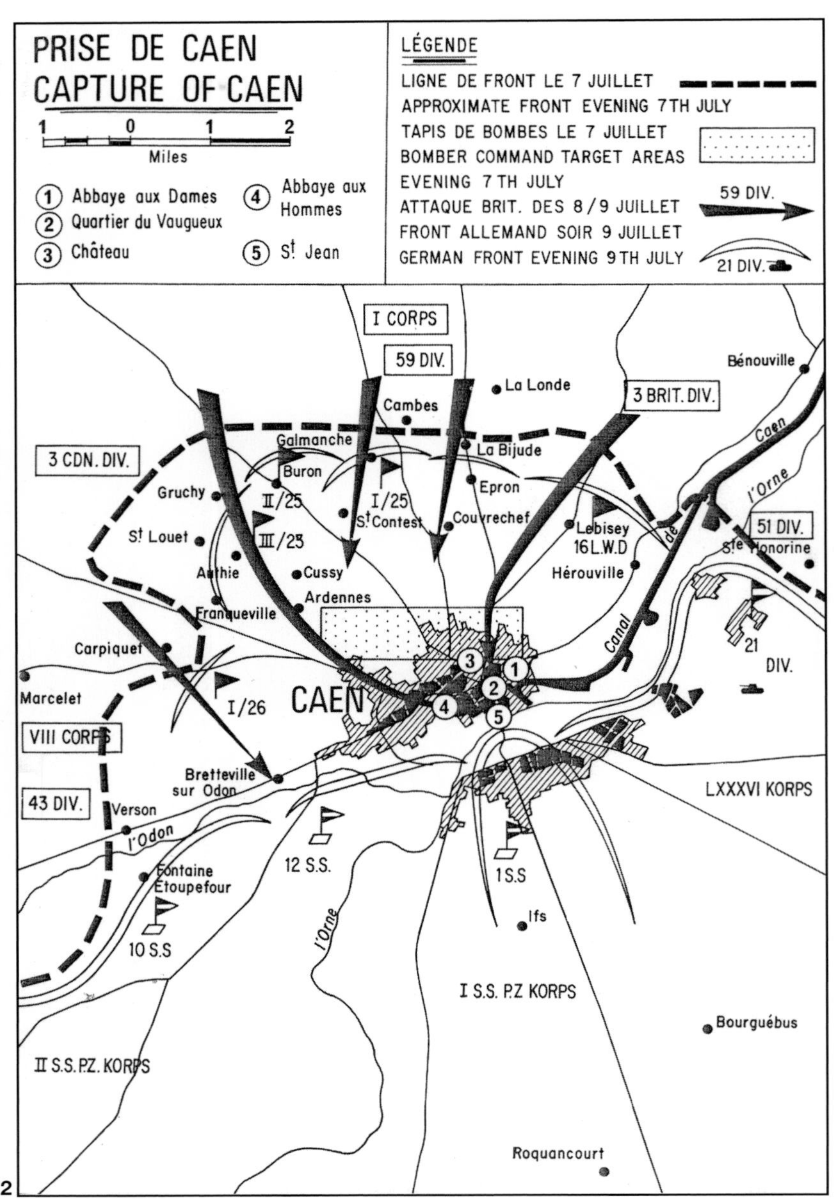

2

1

Caen, the final battle (July 4th-8th)

July 4th, at daybreak. The front line had come to a standstill in front of Caen for over a month when the 3rd Canadian Division moved up to the attack around Carpiquet, outflanking the great Norman city from the west. Operation Windsor is underway. The Winnipegs (RWR) move up from Marcelet, with the Régiment de la Chaudière on their left flank, and the North Shore Regiment closer to the railroad tracks. The tough canadian soldiers advance in open fields facing the german positions of I./26 (Hitlerjugend). Casualties are heavy. The attack goes on throughout July 5th and 6th for the capture of Carpiquet and its airfields where the HJ Grenadiers are well dug in. Their defensive positions and bunkers have to be taken one by one using flame throwers. Very few prisonners are made.

July 7th, north of Carpiquet and the RN 13 heighway, the North Nova Scotia Highlanders send a recon party to Authie. The Canadians lose 20 tanks to a german counter attack led by III./25, 5./12 and 6./12. It preludes a new offensive to the north west of Caen as part of Operation Charnwood. Strong forces are involved : Three infantry divisions, the 3rd Canadian, the 3rd British and the 59th British, supported by many attached units and a great deal of artillery, for a total of 115 000 men agains about 10 000 Germans spread out in this sector. The odds are 11 vs 1 in favor of the Allies. The 3rd Canadian Division resumes its attack towards Buron and the « Abbaye d'Ardenne » on July 8th. A tank battle developps in open fields. The Germans, and the Hitlerjugend's last defenders inside the Abbey must pull back to Caen. The Canadians have unlocked the last obstacle west of Caen. They enter the city on July 9th in the morning. The Germans have withdrawn to the right bank of the Orne river, giving up this part of town as well as the city center. In the meantime, the 3rd British Division comes from the north. With the Germans on the other bank of the Orne river, the liberation of Caen is now a simple affair. But it all ends up in a dead end. The Germans have shortened their defensive lines and still occupy the high grounds above Caen. The great Norman capital is at long last liberated, over a month after D Day. But Montgomery shall therefore strike somewhere else to get out of this no way path.

3

5

4

7

6

8

9

1. July 4th ; this I./26 Hitlerjugend Grenadier has received an face wound and been captured on Carpiquet airfield. He is one of the few prisonners made that day. (PAC.)

2. Following the tough fightings for Carpiquet, the Canadians attack on July 7th and 8th to the north of heighway RN13 with the « Abbaye d'Ardenne » as a main objective in order to seize Caen from the west. The NNSH (North Nova Scotia Highlanders) sends an advanced party to Buron, Authie and Franqueville on July 7th. The german counter attack is led by a grenadier battalion of the Hitlerjugend (III./25) and two companies of Panzer IV, (5./12 and 6./12). The Canadians lose about 20 tanks and pull back beyond Buron, around Les Buissons at nighfall. (Heimdal.)

3. Picture taken on July 9th after the July 8th fightings and showing a knocked out Panther between Authie, Cussy and the « Abbaye d'Ardenne ». It belongs to the tank leader of IIIrd platoon, 1./SS-Pz.Rgt. 12. (PAC.)

4 and **5.** Caen, July 9th. Picture shot from the southern high walls of the castle, where the British soldiers came from, with the city in ruins on the background, and the Saint Pierre church without its steeple and further in the back, the Saint Jean church amidst devastated houses. The Hotel d'Escoville stands on the right side of Saint Pierre church. (IWM and F.J./Heimdal)

6 and **7.** Caen, July 9th, Vaugueux sector. Men of the Anti Tank Platoon, 1st KOSB set up their 6 pounder gun. Oddly enough, this neighborhood has been preserved and only some modern constructions have altered its original aspect. (IWM and F.J./Heimdal.)

8 and **9.** A Humber MK IV of C Squadron, 17th Hussars, 3rd Canadian Division is parked in front of the ruined Hotel D'Escoville (entirely restored after the war), next to the Saint Pierre church downtown Caen. (PAC and F.J./Heimdal.)

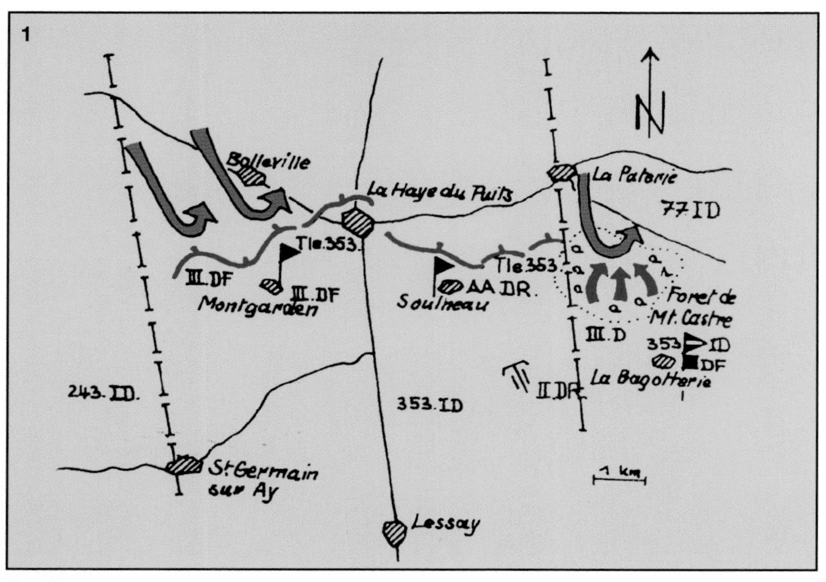

Final battle of La Haye du Puits (July 8-9th)

In this decisive battle, the Germans throw in Kampfgruppe Weidinger, about 4 000 men belonging to the « Das Reich », riflemen, light tanks assault guns and artillery, some of them involved in the Oradour massacre in early June. Some units are in reserve along the front. The counter attack (III./DF) fails. Inside la Haye du Puits, the 353rd ID engineer battalion is only 30 to 40 men strong, accounting for 90% casualties. Its commanding officer, Captain Pillman is listed as MIA. This unit has disintegrated under aerial bombardments and artillery heavy shelling during attacks and counter attacks. One last fight and the survivors will pull out. All approaches to la Haye du Puits have been mined.

On the american side, Major General Middleton draws the conclusion of his VIII Corps operations conducted in the last 5 days ; His casulaties reach 15%. The initial objective, the Lessay sector, is far from achieved since the initial attack only made it about half way to the final goal. But the conquered ground was the most heavily fortified. The ground ahead is flatter and easier to the north of Lessay. The german troops have shown great ability and flawless determination. Among the 15% casualties, 40% account for the infantry. The previous day, the 79th ID lost 1 000 men. The 90th ID has 2 000 casualties on the evening of July 7th after 5 days of fighting for a 6 kilometer advance, or just one casualty for each 3 meters of advance. The 82nd Airborne totally exhausted has been relieved and replaced by the green 8th ID. But the Germans also show great signs of exhaustion in this terrible hedgerow warfare. On July 8th, the 79th ID orders one infantry battalion to move on to La Haye du Puits, supporterd by artillery, mortars and tanks. The US Infantry suffers heavy casualties in front of well dug in german positions but still succeed in infiltrating the northern part of town. The night is enlightened by the fires raging downtown. A company clears the mine fields and the 79th ID hold on to the town by the end of the night. The clearing up takes place on the 9th. Lessay comes next.

1. Kampfgruppe Weidinger counter attacks on each side of La Haye du Puits on July 8th and 9th. (Heimdal according to Munin Verlag.)

2. July 9th, La Haye du Puits overwhelmed by GIs of the 79th ID. A squad carries the different parts of a 80 mm mortar. They return from the front line and move out to Barneville. (NA)

3 and **4.** Riflemen patrol downtown in front of the post office. (NA and E.G./Heimdal.)

79th Infantry Division

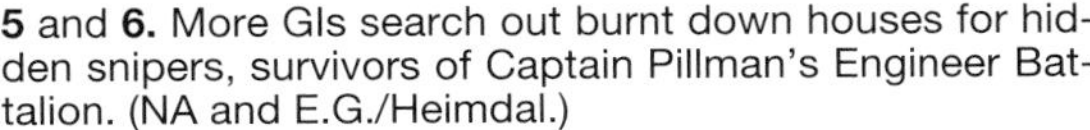

5 and **6.** More GIs search out burnt down houses for hidden snipers, survivors of Captain Pillman's Engineer Battalion. (NA and E.G./Heimdal.)

7. At the outskirts of town, close to the railways, two German prisonners of war watch over their wounded comrade. This takes place on the east of town. (Coll. Heimdal.)

8. July 8th, on Château street, in front of the Café du grand marché, German soldiers just surrendered. They were besieged inside the medieval donjon they are now walking away from. (NA.)

9. Overview of the market place facing north, church in the background.

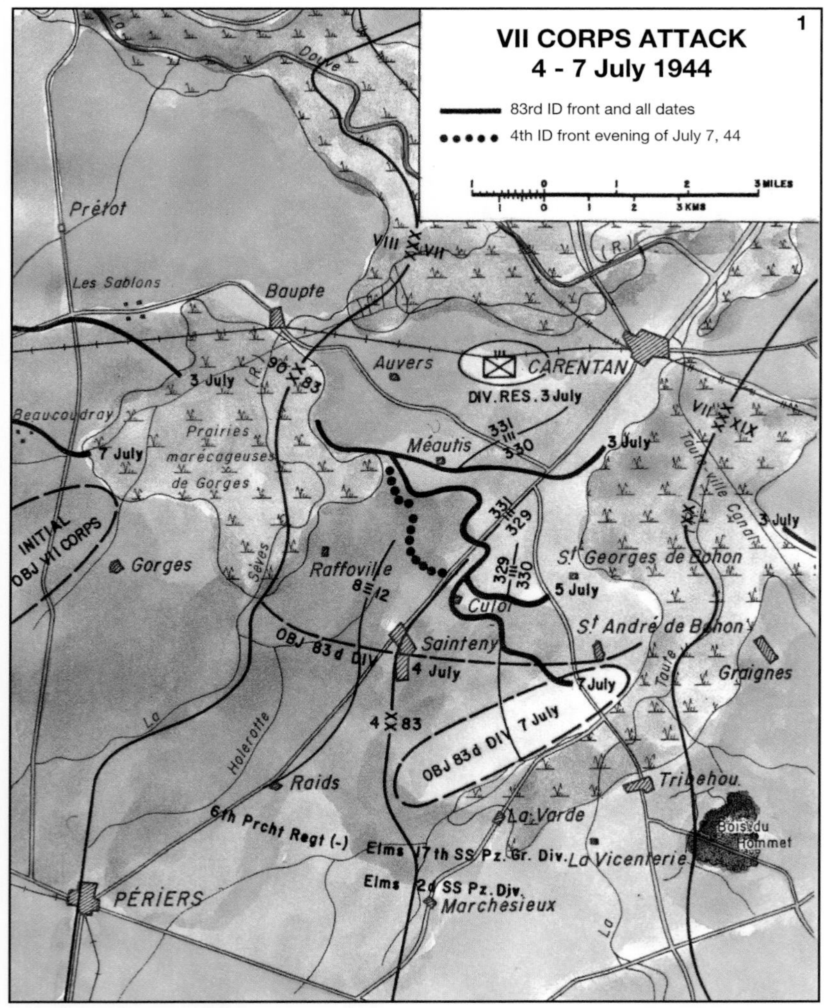

To die for Sainteny (July 4-11th)

Once Carentan finally secured on June 12th (see pages 20-21), the front line remains stable with von der Heydte's parachutists and SS Grenadiers of the « Götz » blocking a narrow « isthmus » of ground between two large marshlands (See map). General Collins can now rely on three infantry divisions (4th ID, 9th ID, 83rd ID). The first two have distinguished themselves in the battle for the Cotentin while the 83rd landed on Omaha Beach June 18th. Collins launches a new attack at dawn on July 4th. The « Götz » with the FJR6 on its left flank is heavily shelled, but the 83rd ID under bad command suffers great losses. Colonel Barndollar, commanding officer of the 331st IR is killed with a bullet through the heart. Casualties are high even though the 330th makes significant progress with a one kilometer gain eastward. The « Götz » also suffers many casualties. On the 5th, Collins still cannot fully deploy his two remaining divisions on such a narrow front. The 83rd loses another 750 men, added to the 1 400 casualties from the previous day in front of Sainteny. On the 6th, the 83rd sector is cut in half in order to allow the 4th ID'engagement on its western flank. But still the 83rd suffers another 700 men, for a total of 3 000 casualties in the battle of Sainteny alone !

But on July 7th, starting at 03.30 hours the 2/117th IR, 30th Infantry Division silently crosses the Vire river at Airel, next to Saint Fromond. The 113th Cavalry Group is hot on its heels. They're only facing weak elements of KG Heintz. On the 8th, tanks from the 3rd Armored are ready to cross the river when KG Wisliceny (made of elements of the 2.SS-Panzer-Division) with about 15 Panzer IV (6./SS-Pz-Rgt. 2) counter attacks. A terrible artillery barrage falls upon the SS troops. The CCB 3rd Armored Division reaches Hauts Vents (See pictures). However, with a crisis looming, the German headquarters has brought in the vicinity the Panzer Lehr Division from the Tilly sur Seules sector. The division gets on the line on july 9th in the same time as Count von der Schulenburg's parachutists of Regiment 13th ; The Count shall be killed on july 14th. The Panzer-Lehr-Division is quick to counter attack into the american beachhead on the 11th heading for Desert and Saint Jean de Daye (See map). Facing a 1 to 6 odds, the PLD makes good progress but is hit around midday by allied fighter-bombers that stop short their offensive towards the Vire-Taute canal. The PLD loses 500 grenadiers and 23 tanks. On the same day, an exhausted « Götz » pulls back to the south of Sainteny...

1. This map shows how narrow the front is south of Carentan, stuck between the Gorges marshes and the Taute marshland. A situation well to the advantage of the german defenders. (US Army and Heimdal.)

2. German parachutists of the Fallschirmjaeger-Regiment 6 in the Méautis sector (South west of Carentan), protected by a hedgerow (Coll. J.Y. Nasse.)

3. Young (17 to 20 years old) parachutists move out to the front ; they belong to the Fallschirmjaeger-Regiment 13 (Count von der Schulenburg) in the Champs de Losques sector on july 9th. (Coll. A. Pipet/Heimdal.)

4. Map showing the operations west of the Vire river, bypassed on july 7th in Airel by the 30th ID and the 3rd AD. This offensive will stall in front of the Panzer-Lehr Division coming to the rescue from Tilly sur Seulles. (US Army/Heimdal.)

5. Columns of Sherman tanks from D Company 33rd Armored Regiment, 3rd Armored Division move out to the front in the Saint Fromond sector on July 9th, ,bypassing knocked out tanks belonging to the « Das Reich ». (NA.)

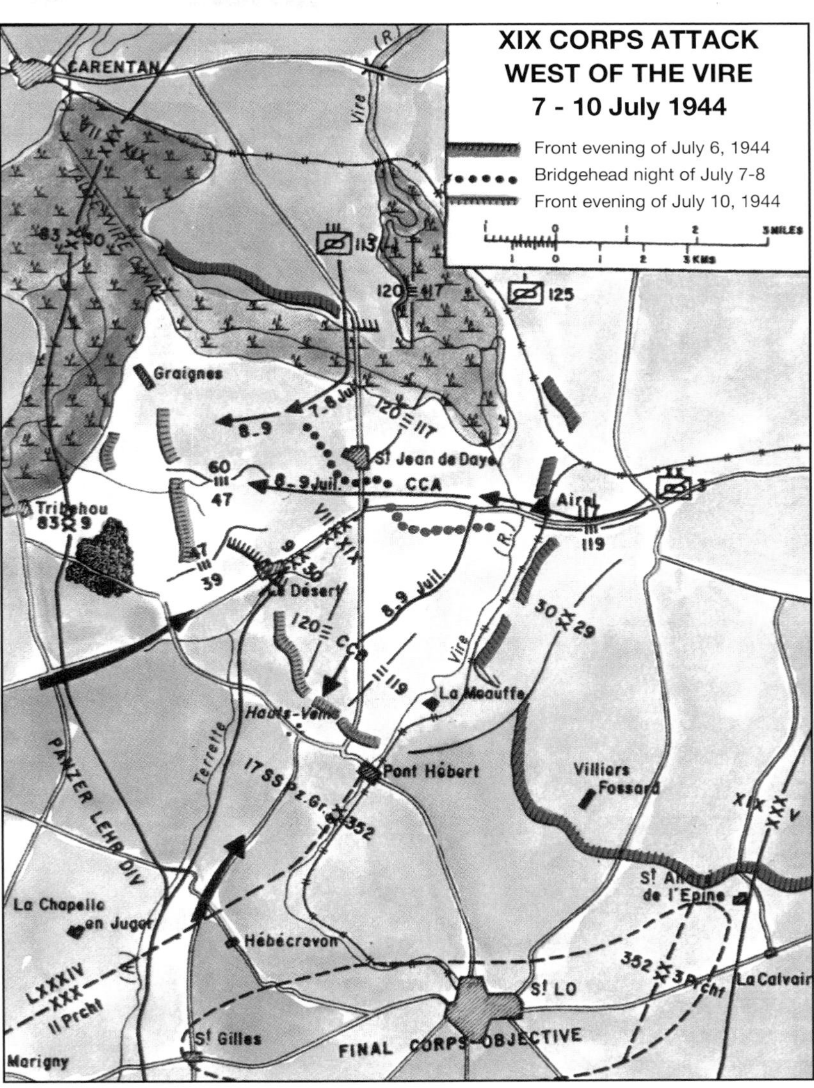

6. July 11th 1944. Saint Fromond area. Tanks and vehicles of the 33rd Armored Regiment, 3rd AD stack up on a muddy road. A few hundred yards ahead their comrades fight off a German counter attack lead by the Panzer-Lehr Division and coming from Hauts Vents. This Stuart light tank belongs to C Company, 33rd Armored Regiment and is named « Carol ». (NA/.Heimdal.)

7 and **8.** Downtown Sainteny, the church lies in ruins after the fighting. Then and now. (NA and E.G./Heimdal.)

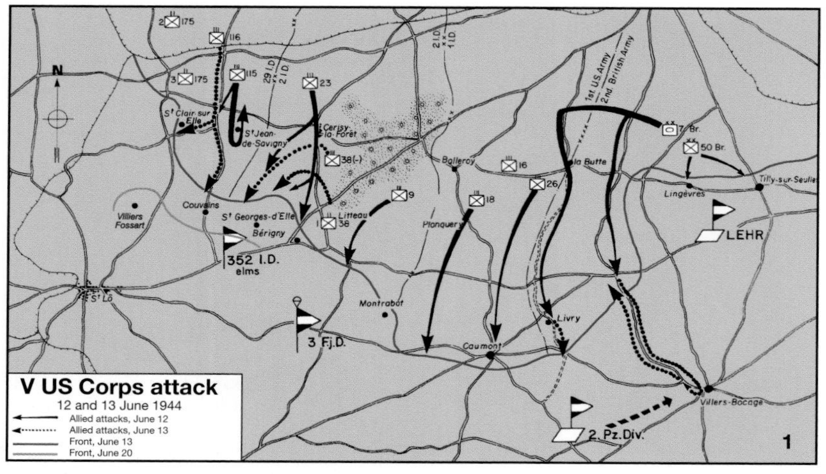

Hell in hedgerow country, north of Saint Lô

In the south of Omaha Beach, the three divisions that landed here made initially good progress against a weak german opposition (mostly remnants of the 352.ID – see pages 8 and 9). As early as June 13th elements of the 1st Infantry division (The Big Red One) reaches the Caumont L'Eventé sector (a strategic high ground) allowing a British armoured division (the 7th Armoured division) a bold overlapping move to Villers Bocage that unfortunately ended in disaster (See the Villers Bocage chapter). On the western side, the 29th Infantry Division crosses the Elle river on the 12th and 13th of June at the high cost of 547 casualties. In spite of the loss of General der Artillerie Erich Marcks (CO of the LXXXIV. AK) killed June 12th by a fighter-bomber, the german front tightens up with on rushing reinforcements : the 2. Panzer Division in the Caumont sector, and a parachutist division, the 3. Fallschirmjaeger Division north of Saint Lô. So it is that on June 20th, following 7 days of tough fighting, the 29th Infantry Division (the Blue and grey) gets stuck south west of Couvain, about 6 kilometers from Saint Lô, facing the Villiers-Fossard saliant where each hedgerow turns into a bloody battle and gives this part of Normandy its well deserved nickname, « Hedgerow hell ». A merciless battle rages on for a whole month. A violent storm destroys the Omaha Beach artificial harbor and slows down considerably ammunition supplies and reinforcements, to the point where no serious offensive can be undertaken.

So it is that a month after D Day, Saint Lô still appears totally out of Allies reach. The Germans hang on by the skin of their teeth to the surrrounding hills, mostly on hill 122 to the north and 192 to the north east. Built on top of rocky heights, Saint Lô, capital of the Manche Department, a former fortified medieval city above the Vire river, is naturally protected by a line of hills which must be taken prior to entering the city. On the northern side, Hill 122 becomes the 29th Infantry Division's objective. To the east, Hill 192 is first covered by the 2nd Infantry Division, then the 1st ID all the way to Caumont. On July 12th, the 29th ID, supported by the green 35th ID (landed on July 9th) faces Hill 122, a german bastion backed by the Carillon strongpoint. The division makes slow progress, mostly to the east on the Martainville ridge, at a horrendous price of 1 000 men lost within 2 days. On that day, the 2nd ID suffers 69 killed, 328 woounded and 8 missing. Hedgerow country is truely hell.

1. V Corps attack on June 12th and 13th. The First Infantry Division achieves the deepest penetration, all the way to Caumont-L'Eventé and the high grounds. But the front shall freeze up to that point until August because of strong resistance from the 2nd Panzer Division. The 29th and 2nd ID crossed the Elle river and advanced a couple of miles before heading into strong German reinforcements, particularly the 3. Fallschirmjaeger-Division. The Germans sink deep into hedgerow country and offer stiff opposition for every inch of ground. (Heimdal).

2. Hell on earth, July 6th. The battle for the hedgerows is carried at platoon or squad level. A never ending, exhausting and confusing kind of warfare. An american patrol ambushed a german party who fled leaving behind an automatic weapon, an MG 42. The GI's attempt to neutralize the opposition. This soldier raises his helmet trying to attract enemy fire in order to pin point german positions. (Coll. Heimdal.)

3. US outpost in Saint Lô sector. (Coll. Heimdal.)

4. July 11th, a T5 carries on his jeep Private Vincent Lucas from Braddock, Pennsylvania. Braddock was wounded by a mine and was taken to the aid station. The stenciled 29th ID patch can be seen on the driver's helmet. (DAVA.)

5. Medics take care of a wounded GI whose wrist has been hit. (DAVA.)

6. Engineers and communication men string telephone wires along a ditch, on July 13th. The battle for Saint Lô is underway. (DAVA/Heimdal.)

7. On daylight moves, military police of the 3. Fallschirmjaeger-Division in this folliage covered Stöwer vehicle, are on constant watch out for Allied fighter-bombers coming down from the skies to wreck havoc on the convoys. (BA.)

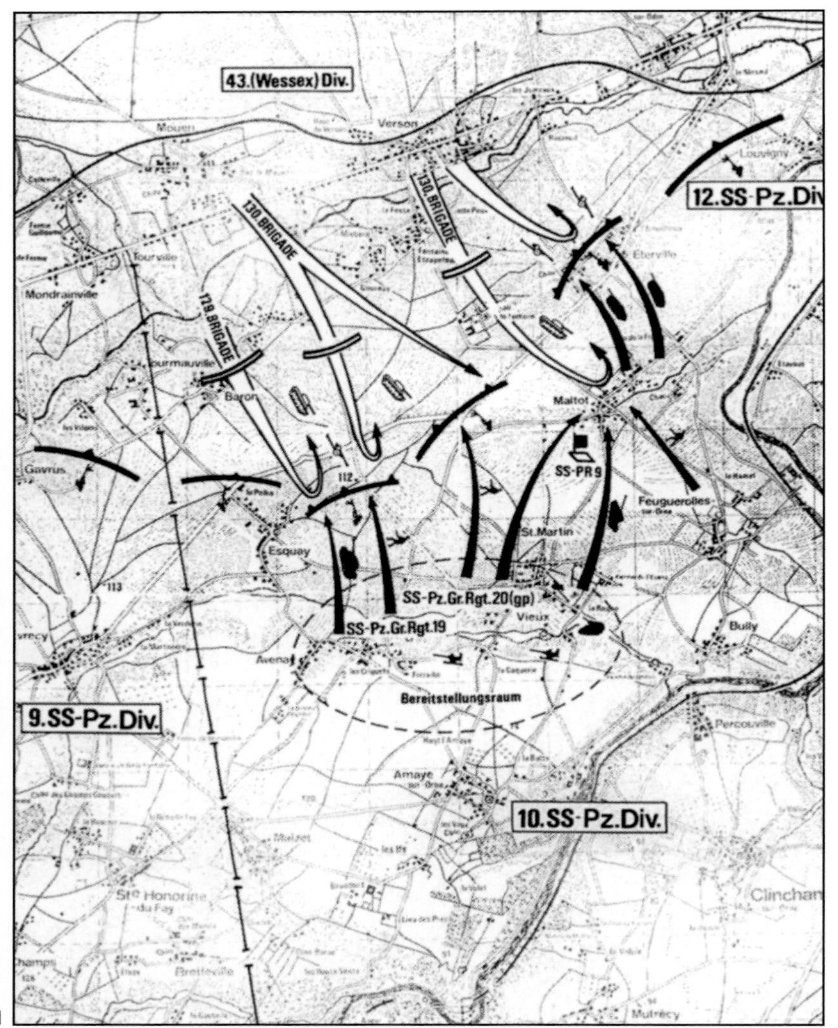

Hell on Hill 112 (July 10th-16th)

Saturday 1st of July. Following the failure of operation Epsom, the Hohenstaufen launches a new attack on Rauray. The attack fails. The SS division is relieved and replaced by an Infantry division, the 277. ID. The front line stabilizes into a trench warfare. But after the fall of Caen on July 8th, Montgomery renews his attacks in this sector following the same objectives as per Operation Epsom, in order to find a way out of the Caen dead end. Called operation Jupiter, it starts off on a Monday July 10th at dawn with a single division, the 43rd Wessex Division. The Fontaine-Etoupefour castle is taken from elements of the Frundsberg Division (I./22) by the 130 Brigade. But the roughest moments occur on the right wing (west) for the 129 Brigade, facing Hill 112, as the Germans get reinforcements : Tiger tanks from the s. SS-Panzer-Abteilung 102. The 4 Dorset seizes Eterville, the Hampshires head for Maltot. The 15th Scottish Division gives support to the left flank. But on Hill 112 as well as at Maltot, the assault is repulsed by Tiger tanks and SS-Oscha. Will Fey distinguishes himself during the fighting.

At dawn on Sunday July 11th, the Frundsberg Division renews its attack towards Maltot and Eterville, and the Fontaine castle. In the meantime, the Hohenstaufen counter attacks on Hill 112 where its 3./19 suffers heavy casualties. Operation Jupiter is a failure. Hill 112 changes hands repeatedly but shall never really fall into British hands ; They hold the northern slopes while the Germans hang on to the southern side. Hill 112, truly a Norman « Verdun ».

When he hears about the american plan to breakthrough (Operation Goodwood), Montgomery tries to outspeed them by launching here another offensive called operation Greenline, starting July 15th at 21.00 hours (XII Corps with the 15th Scottish Division, the 53rd Welsh Division and Churchill tanks of the 34th Army Tank Brigade). This first night attack used flak searchlights aiming at the clouds in order to create artificial lighting. Esquay falls. But at dawn, July 16th, the 10. SS-Pz.-Div. « Frundsberg » counter attacks with the help of elements of the Hohenstaufen called to the rescue. The British onslaught is stopped cold. The war of attrition goes on without any significant success. The Germans finally give up Hill 112 to the 53rd Division during their general withdrawal on August 4th.

1. This map shows the attacks of the 43rd Wessex Division on July 10th and the successful counter attacks launched by the 9.SS-Panzer-Division « Hohenstaufen » on July 11th on Hill 112 (SS-Pz. Gren.-Rgt 19 backed by tanks of 1./SS-Pz.regt. 9) while SS-Pz.Gren.-Rgt. 20 counter attack from Vieux on Maltot, then Eterville, supported by Panzers from IInd Battalion. (HF/Heimdal map.)

2. SS-Oberführer Heinz Harmel, Frundsberg commanding officer aboard a Befehls-Funkpanzer in Feuguerolles on July 10th. He leads as close as possible from the front. (Bayeux Musée Mémorial.)

3. Fontaine-Etoupefour castle, command post of II./22 falls on July 10th. (E.G. /Heimdal.)

4

EIN MITTELPUNKT DER SCHLACHT SÜDLICH CAEN

HÖHE 112

Wie bei Verdun: Wochenlang geht der Kampf um einen einzigen Hügel

So sieht die vorderste Front aus

Mühsam wurde ein Loch in den steinigen Boden gewühlt, dann mit Bohlen und Steinen abgedeckt. In diesem Loch lebt, schläft und kämpft der deutsche Grenadier

Das ist die vielumkämpfte Höhe 112 bei Caen

„Tascheninhalt vorzeigen!"

5

4. Tiger tank 211, belonging to 2nd Company (SS-Hstuf. Endemann commanding). This company of the s.SS-Panzer-Abteilung 102 will fight on Hill 112 on July 10th with 1st Company to the right, between Maltot and the hilltop. (Thierry Vallet.)

5. The Hamburger Illustrierte, a hambourg based magazine in the summer of 1944 mentions the Hill 112 fighting. Clearly visible is a Panzer IV of 5th Company, Frundsberg tank division.

6. Soon after the fighting two Caen inhabitants, Serge Varin and a friend stroll through the battlefield and shoot this remarkable picture on Hill 112. We can see wrecked Sherman tanks in the Great Orchard, most probably belonging to the Royal Scots Geys who backed up the resistance from 5 DCLI near Hill 112. (S. Varin/Heimdal.)

7. This other picture shows trees in the Great Orchard torn apart by artillery shells, a vision reminiscent of the « great war ». The Germans shall call this place the « half tree wooden patch ». (S. Varin/Heimdal.)

7

6

1

2

A base for a new offensive (July 10-13)

For the american foot soldier, the first two weeks of fighting in the Cotentin hedgerow country are demoralizing. The taking of Saint Lô on July 19th completes and terminates the First Army offensive launched on july 2nd, and which was supposed to secure a good launching base for an even more decisive battle on a Lessay/Caumont L'Eventé line of departure.

But this offensive lead by First Army and an dozen Divisions only gained 7 miles (11 kilometers) west of the Vire river. As a result, the Germans have withdrawn behind a new line of resistance, and this withdrawal in good order does not show any sign of a quick break out in the german front. To gain this 11 kilometer foothold, First Army has suffered 40 000 casualties (Killed, wounded and missing), 90% being riflemen. At the end of the offensive, some infantry companies only account for the size of a platoon. Veteran and author of a history of the 329th IR, 83rd ID, Raymond J Goguen wrote : *« We won the battle, but considering the high price in american lives, we lost. »* Companies will be brought back at full strength (which will not be the case on the german side), but with green troops who, in turns will pay dearly for their lack of experience. The american rifleman, isolated among dense and hostile hedgerow country will fall victim of combat fatigue and field hospitals treat 25 to 30% of such cases. The american GI cannot see the end of this nightmare and feel disheart-ed : *« We could see the war lasting for twenty years »* Worse even, tension rises among the Allies, with Americans giving it all and suffering already 39 341 casualties, when the Anglo-Canadians « only » have 22 208. The British appear to fight a more careful war.

Lt Gen Bradley knows it. He also acknowleges that the german front is nearing the breaking point after all this heavy fighting and little replacements. As early

2bis

3

as July 10th, Montgardon and La haye du Puits fall into american hands, Sainteny on the next day. A beach head is established at Saint-Fromond but Saint Lô will not fall until July 19th. This base settled, and the end of marshlands will therefore allow the start of a large offensive on a bigger scale. Conceived on the 11th, the idea becomes a master plan for First Army on the 13th with the German withdrawal. This offensive bears the name of a recoiling snake, ready to strike, Cobra. The Americans shall fight with a favorable ratio of 5 versus 1.

1. American artillery plays a decisive role in progressively crushing the german front. It keeps on pounding even when Allied air power is grounded by bad weather. Shown here is a 9th Infantry Division battery in action near saint Jean de Daye on July 13th. These are 105 mm Howitzers HM2 of the 84th Field Artillery battalion (one of the four battalions attached to the 9th ID) shooting from under camouflage nettings. Hidden along a hedgerow, they open fire on german defenses from 2 000 yards behind the front line. (DAVA)

2. This shot is from the rear end of one of these Howitzers as the casing is being ejected. The gunner wears the division insignia on his sleeve. That same insignia appears on hemet « 2bis ». (DAVA and private coll.)

3. Gunners from that same battery remove shells and cases from the ammunition boxes and assemble complete shells ready to fire. (DAVA/Coll. Heimdal)

4. Fighter-bombers are deadly weapons for defending Germans constantly looking for camouflage. Here are two wrecked Panthers from the 1st tank company of the PLD after the july 11th attack from Hauts-Vents. They fell to CCB, 3rd Armored Division. Picture shot on July 13th. (DAVA/coll. Heimdal.)

5. Another tank from the same company knocked out on the 11th by a 3rd Armored tank Destroyer. The burnt out body of one of the tank crew lies on the chassis. Picture taken on the 19th. (DAVA/Heimdal.)

6. Men of the 337th Antiaircraft battalion, a flak unit attached to the 4th ID opens up with their quad 50 (12,7 mm). Mounted on a half track, it operates in the Sainteny sector on July 12th. (DAVA/Heimdal.)

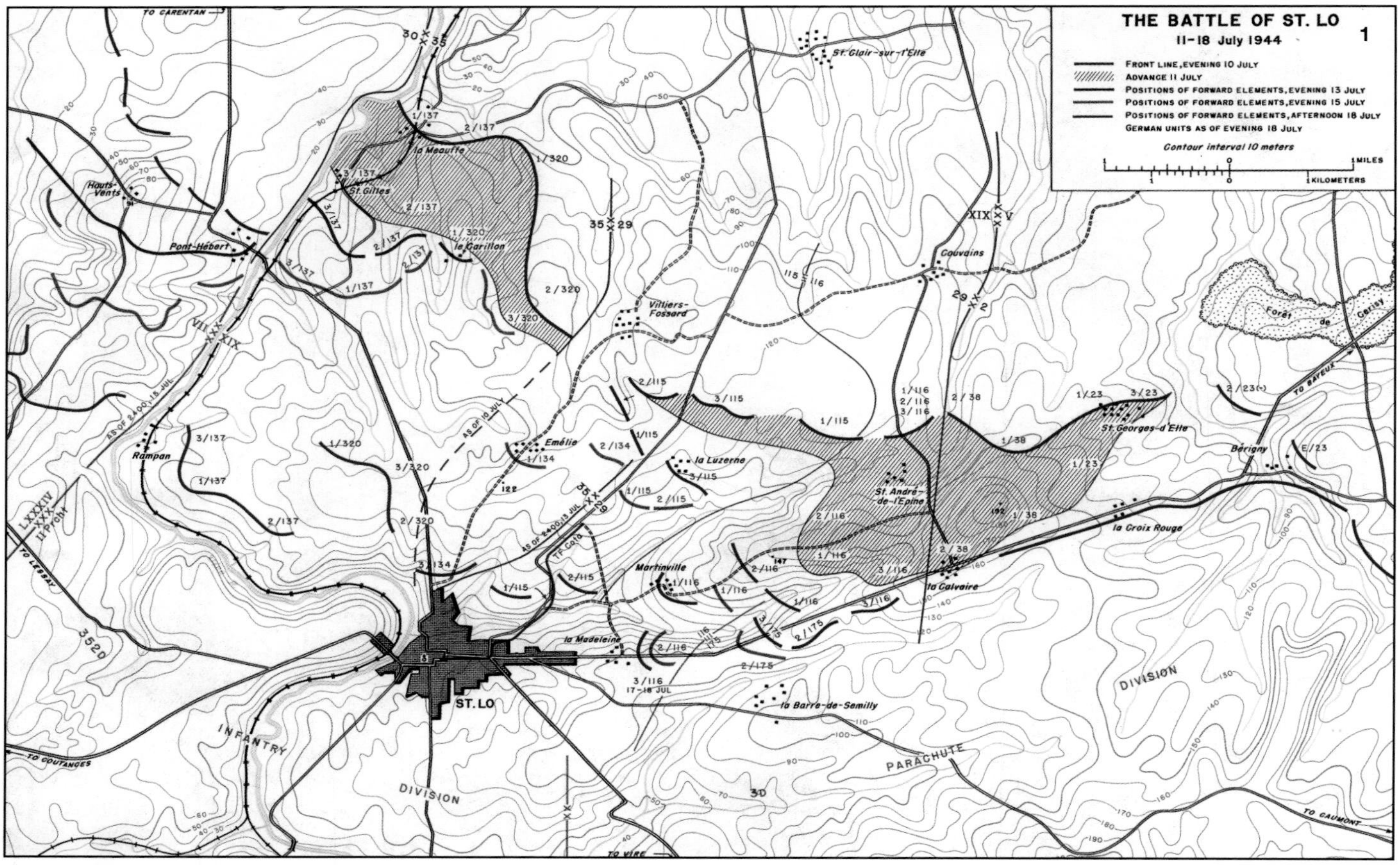

THE BATTLE OF ST. LO
11–18 July 1944 1

- FRONT LINE, EVENING 10 JULY
- ADVANCE 11 JULY
- POSITIONS OF FORWARD ELEMENTS, EVENING 13 JULY
- POSITIONS OF FORWARD ELEMENTS, EVENING 15 JULY
- POSITIONS OF FORWARD ELEMENTS, AFTERNOON 18 JULY
- GERMAN UNITS AS OF EVENING 18 JULY

Contour interval 10 meters

2

3

The battle for Saint Lô (July 13-18)

The terrible hedgerow country battle to reach Saint Lô goes on raging by July 13th when the 35th ID short of experience pushes towards Hill 122, supported by the 30th ID shooting from the western banks of the Vire river. The area is defended by a german parachutist corps, Gen. Lt Meindl's II.Fallschirmjaeger Korps, beefed up by the remnants of three infantry divisions, (KG 266, KG 352 and KG 353) and a division of parachutists, the 3. Fallschirmjaeger-Division. On July 14th, the joint effort by all the american divisions and a powerful artillery barrage break the german front ; in two days, KG 352 suffers 840 wounded from shell fire and a great number of dead. On july 15th, the 35th ID keeps up its attacking pace and overrun the Germans east of Mesnil-Rouxelin, and threatens Saint George Montcocq, a mere two kilometers north of Saint Lô. Following a rainfall of steel and fire, Hill 122 is finally taken. Its defenders are on the run. In the center front, the 29th ID advances slowly and reaches the la Madeleine crossroads east of Saint Lô under the direct threat of the Martainville ridge. Major Bingham's battalion is surrounded.

On July 16th, the german front is about to collapse. On the 17th, the II.Fj-Korps left flank has broken under heavy pressure by the 35th ID, but the glory to enter Saint Lô befalls upon the 29th ID. As early as July 18th, Major General Corlett (CO XIX Corps) orders Major General Gerhardt its commanding officer to send a Task Force downtown to secure the city. This Task Force is commanded by Brig. Gen. Cota made famous by his feat of arms at Omaha Beach on D-Day. The Task Force leaves La Luzerne at 15.10 hours and enters Saint Lô from the north east (the actual D 6). At 19.00 hours, the devastated city is in american hands. Major Howie is killed while attacking the La Madeleine ridge with his 3/116 ; his men carry his

XIX Corps

35th ID

29th ID

body to the Sainte Croix church downtown Saint Lô. He's from then on the « Major of Saint Lô ». On July 19th, the 35th ID also enters Saint Lô, the « capital of ruins », to relieve the exhausted GI's of the Blue and Gray Division. This victory clears the left flank of First army and paves the way for operation « Cobra ».

1. The final battle for Saint Lô, from July 11th til July 18th. The blue area shows the advance as per July 11th. To the north facing Le Carillon, advances the 35th ID towards Hill 122. In the center, heading for the Martinville ridge is the 29th ID and to the east the 2nd ID holds Hill 192. (US Army.)

2. July 19th, Task Force Charlie enters saint Lô and reaches the la Bascule crossroads, a road hub network connecting the Bayeux, Isigny and Torigni heighways to downtown Saint Lô. Troops and tanks converge and take a right turn for the City center.

3. Foot soldiers and armored vehicles move out among rubbles between Place sainte Croix and the City center. (DAVA.)

4. The city is in ruins, constantly bombed since June 6th. The local population suffers heavy losses. Here is the la Dollée neighborhood to the north of the upper part of Saint Lô. (NA.)

5. Another color photo taken from the la Dollée area and looking uptown where the mutilated Notre Dame church tower still stands. (NA.)

6. From that church tower looking east and the Vire river. Saint Lô shall be named « the capital of ruins ». The city is badly mauled. Saint Lô suffered the greatest devastation among all Norman cities, along with Le Havre, destroyed at 77% (a number reaching 92% when reconstruction started). 326 inhabitants oficially died during the bombing. (NA.)

1

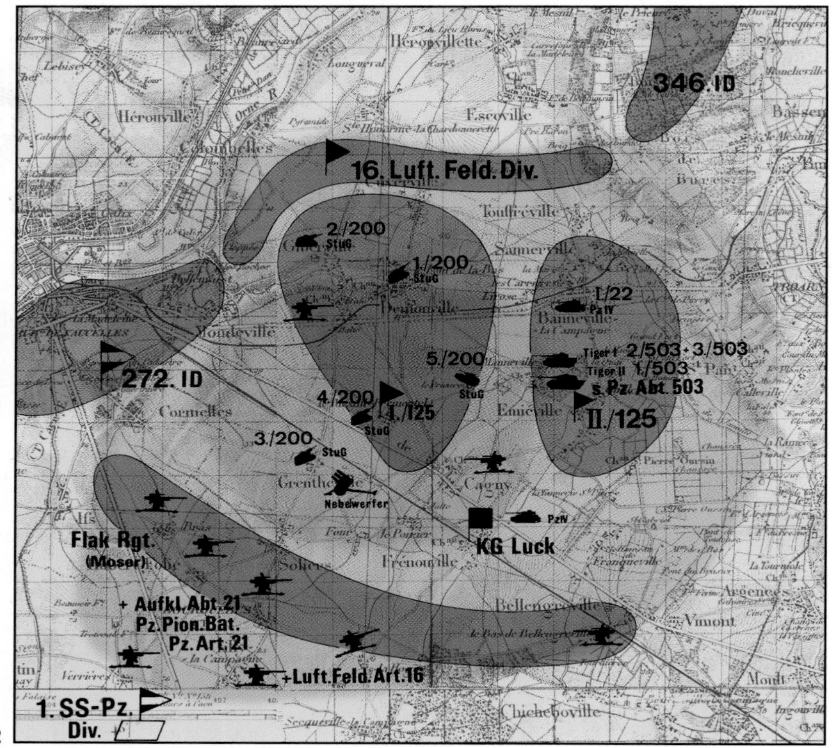

2

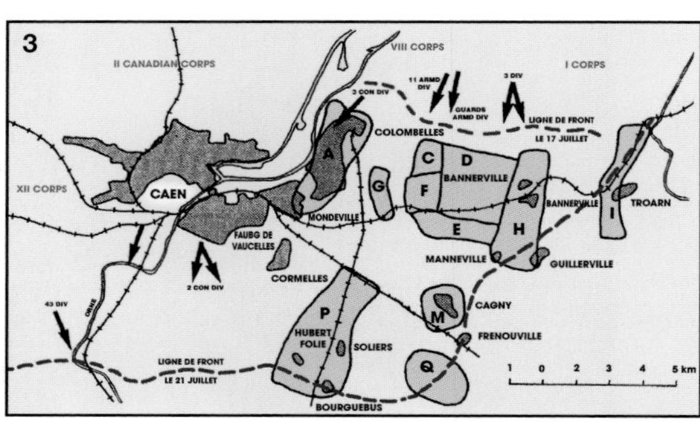

1. Vehicles of the attacking force assemble within the airborne beachhead east of the Orne river. One can see on this picture shot next to Pegasus bridge in the background, dozens of Cromwell et TD tanks from the Welsh Guards, Guards Armoured Division. A great score of these tanks will be out of action by the end of the fighting. (IWM.)

2. This map shows the german positions as they come under severe bombardments ; of special interest is the front line positions of 272.ID, 16.LFD, 346.ID. Kampfgruppe Luck comes in second row, with the artillery forces spread out along the Bourguébus ridge. The orange part indicates areas submitted to the bombardments. (Heimdal.)

3. Bombing map.

4. German counter attack and stabilisation of the front lines ; Peiper's I./SS-Pz. Rgt 1 Panther tanks counter attack at the bottom of Bourguébus ridge. This move is supported by StuGs from the 21.PD. On the west flank, men from III./1 LAH reinforce the german positions in Bras and Hubert-Folie. Standing in front of Bourguébus are the Grenadiers from 3./1. The British assault is broken, particularly because of accurate fire from the 8,8 Flak. Though destroyed by 16.00 hours, these guns inflicted heavy casualties with their flanking fire on the british columns. It was then considered suicidal to go on with an attack that had already cost close to 200 tanks. (Heimdal).

Operation « Goodwood » July 17-20)

With Caen liberated on July 10th, the Allied beachhead remains quite narrow and Monty is way behind schedule in his Master plan ; By D+20, June 26th, he was supposed to have reached Falaise. Caen is a dead end. And the RAF is raising more and more criticism against his leadership. On June 27th, Air Chief Marshall Tedder, Einsenhower'sAid at SHAEF and Air Vice Marshal Conningham, Commanding 2nd TAF both asked Churchill for his head. His lack of decision making ability is also criticised on July 7th by Eisenhower. On a July 10th conference, First Army Boss Bradley unveils the coming plan for a new offensive, Cobra. Right away, Monty tries to overcome Bradley and let Eisenhower know on July 12th that Dempsey, Second Army CO is attacking west of the Orne river from the Airborne beachhead, with Falaise as a main objective.

But this is exactly where Rommel had expected an attack, on flat ground favorable to tanks. His defense is three lines deep (see map), with infantry (272.ID, 16. LFD, 346.ID) on the first line, Kampfgruppe Luck, elements of the 21.PD commanded by Major Hans von Luck with its attached grenadiers regiment, Pz. Gren. Rgt 125, supported by the self propelled guns of StuG.Abt. 200 and Tiger tanks of s.Pz-Abt 503 as a second line of resistance. The third line is made of artillery and 88 mm guns of Flak-Rgt Moser. Monty on the other side is short on infantry ; on the line is his VIII Corps, with 1 000 tanks and three armoured divisions (Guards Armoured Division, 7th Armoured Division and 11th Armoured Division). The armored leading effort is supported on the eastern side by the I Corps, and to the west by the II Canadian Corps. These units get set on July 17th on their base of departure.

On July 18th, 942 British bombers reach their objectives at 05.35 hours. They inflict horrendous damages to the Germans. Panzers are thrown up into the

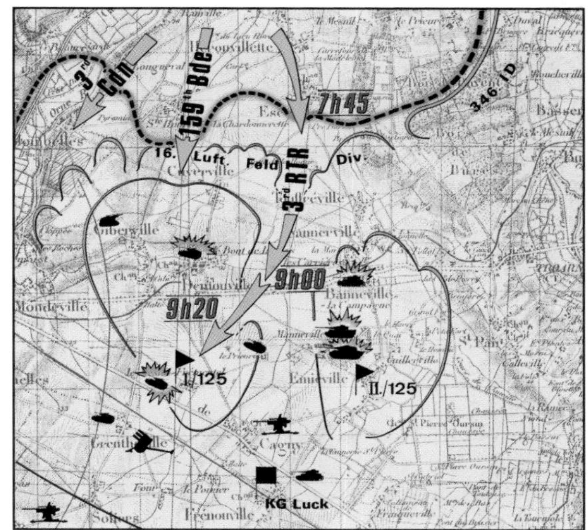

5

air by concussion and even heavy Tiger tanks assembled in the Chateau de Manneville estate are turned upside down. The 16. Luftwaffen-Feld-Division is annihilated. Tanks with 3rd Royal Tank Regiment (11th Armoured Division) in the lead break easily through the first german line of resistance from 07.45 hours on. They fight off some StuG and by 10.15 hours come under flat trajectory flanking fire from a 88 Flak battery. Major von Luck is directing fire from the north of Cagny. The tanks suffer heavy losses and must cope with Major Becker's StuGs.

At noon, the British second Army headquarters receives an enthusiastic report ; tanks from the 11th Armoured Division are closing on Bourguébus ridge. But on the battle field, situation appears to be quite different. The infantry is lagging in the rear, trying to defeat unexpected pockets of resistance in Démouville. 3rd RTR is stalled in front of Hubert-Folie, at the most extreme point of the British advance. The 11th AD was to reach Bretteville sur Laize, while the Guards were supposed to take Vimont and the 7th AD was to head for Falaise. Its attack finally occurs at 17.00 hours, when at the same time, the Leibstandarte counterattacks. Peiper's Panther tank battalion (I.SS-Pz-Rgt 1) pushes the 23rd Hussars back. The II Canadian Corps launches an attack (operation Atlantic) on the west flank and I Corps on the eastern flank, stopped cold by the 346 ID. The operation is a failure. It still goes on another day on the 19th with casualty rate rising for the British whose losses top 314 tanks out of 1 000. On July 20th, rainfall definitely puts a term to their offensive. A brilliant defensive victory for the Germans that swedish army cadets shall study after the war. Monty from then on needs a strong polish and canadians support to make up for his heavy losses.

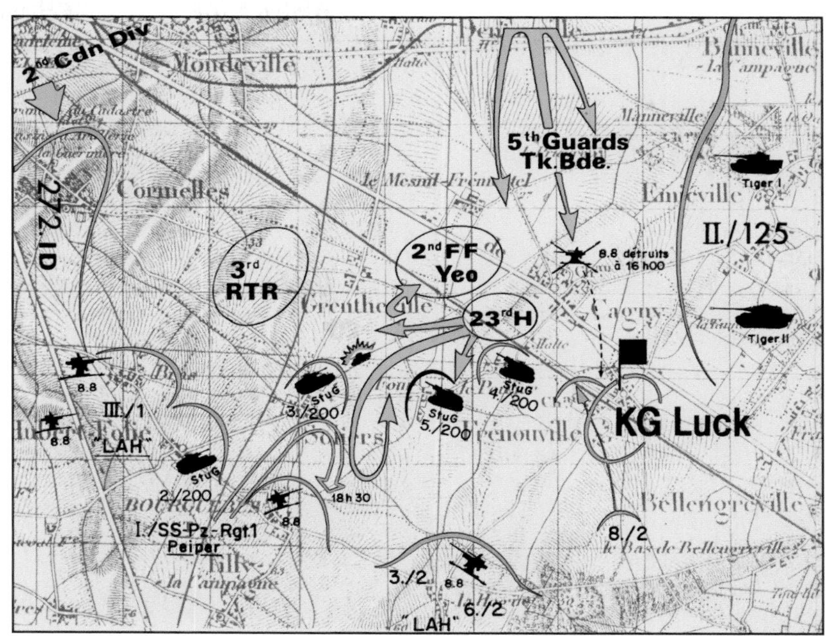

4

6

5. The assault. Besides german losses on the front lines and to the flanks, the British tanks attack is running behind schedule. The crossing of british mine fields has been slow and the Démouville defenders as well as a railroad track have also added to the delay. (Heimdal map).

6. Tiger tank belonging to 2nd Company, s.Panzer-Abteilung 503. Number « 213 » stuck deep into the Manneville castle ditch as a result of the bombardments. The crew made good their escape. (CA via P. Wirton)

8

7 and **8.** Assault gun from 2./200, 2nd battery Sturmgeschütz-Abteilung 200 knocked out of action in Giberville village. This is a 10,5 cm FH 18/40 auf Geschützwagen 38 H (f) that set the adjoining house on fire. The building has since been renovated but still bears remainders of the 1944 impacts. (IWM and E.G./ Heimdal.)

7

1. Based on their experiences in combat at Villiers-Fossard and Hauts-Vents, the engineers of the 3rd Armored Divisions, men from the 23rd Armored Engineer battalion come up with « dragon teeth » welded to the front of tanks ; the « hedgecutter » tank is born. This effective addition was built from salvaged german beach obstacles, in abundance on the coast line. It was both simple and ingenious. Here in action is a Sherman tank of the 3rd Armored Division with its « hedgecutter ». (DAVA/Heimdal.)

2. Hedgerows raised major problems to the american tank units. Besides the « hedgecutters », the US engineers came up with Tank-dozers, equipped with a bull-dozer blade ; here is one of those used by the 3rd Armored Division. (DAVA/Heimdal.)

3. July 24th, on the eve of the assault, artillery and mortars get ready to participate in the crushing of the german lines. Mortarmen of the 87th heavy mortar battalion unload from a tracked vehicle M29 Weasel cases of 4,2 inches shells (just over 100 mm shells...) (Heimdal.)

Cobra gets underway (July 14-24)

In order to launch this offensive, the First Army can from now on rely on certain advantages. The infantry has made great progress in its anti tank warfare. Thanks to the bazooka, the rifleman is no longer helpless to fight off tanks. And as early as the 5th of July, the 79th ID has conceived the « hedgecutter », improved by the ingenuity of Sergeant Curtis G Curlin Jr of the 102nd Cavalry Reconnaissance squadron. Huge steel teeth are fixed to the front end of tanks to cut off hedges. They are built out of beach obstacles set up by the Germans.These tanks are called « Rhinoceros », or simply « Rhinos ». The 23rd Armored Engineer Battalion, 3rd Armored Division also claims to have invented the device. At the time of operation Cobra, three out of five tanks are equipped with hedgecutters. To keep the device a secret, Bradley forbides the use of these tanks prior to the operation.

Four armored divisions and four infantry divisions have come as reinforcements. The First Army is now made out of four army corps for a total of 15 divisons. Major General Collins VII Corps spearheads the attack with great reinforcements. Two infantry divisions make out the first line (9th ID and 30th ID), soon to be bypassed by two armored divisions (3rd AD and 2nd AD) ; and two more infantry divisions (1st ID and 4th ID). VII Corps relies to the east, in the Saint Lô sector on the XIX and V Corps. To the west, Major General Midleton's VIII Corps will join up the offensive with two more armored divisions (4th and 6th AD) and four infantry divisions.

These considerable forces are to charge through a 700 yards wide and 2 500 yards deep gap opened by a massive bombardment. This carpet bombing is supposed to crush the german defenders all along the front line in the Panzer-Lehr Division sector, or what's left of it, 5 000 men and 40 tanks, remnants of the FJR. 13, and Kampfgruppe Heintz. It is also meant to destroy all german communication lines, reduce their reserves and annihilate the germans soldiers will to fight through sheer terror. On July 19th, Bradley is in England to take care of this aerial support ; he gets a total of 3 000 planes engaged in the operation. 1 800 heavy bombers shall saturate the area with bombs for an hour, 80 minutes before the start of the attack. 350 fighter bombers will take part of the attack with mission to strafe and bomb the line of advance for 20 minutes. 10 minutes later, 396 medium bomber will drop their loads on the southern edge of the area for 45 minutes. The whole operation should be conducted under the surveilliance of 500 fighter planes to protect this great aerial armada. In order to exploit the situation, Lt General Patton is expected to throw his Third army into the breach. His forward echelon is already close to Valognes. But General Montgomery also wants his own offensive ; on july 18th, he launches Goodwood.

4 and **5.** July 23rd, soldiers of the 4th ID moving up the front lines ; a norman farm lady watches as they walk by the La maison Basset farm in Hommet-d'Arthenay. Now and then. GIs follow the one way sign. (DAVA/Heimdal.)

6. This diagram shows the locations of american units prior to the offensive. The major part played by VII Corps appears quite obvious, with its 2 infantry divisions supported by 2 armored divisions, the 3rd and 2nd, backed up by 2 more infantry divisions in reserve, the 1st and 4th ID. To the west, the other arm of the pincer is made up of 4 infantry divisions, the 79th, 8th, 90th and 83rd, with an armored division for the breakthrough, the 4th AD, and the 6th AD in Corps reserve. (Heimdal map).

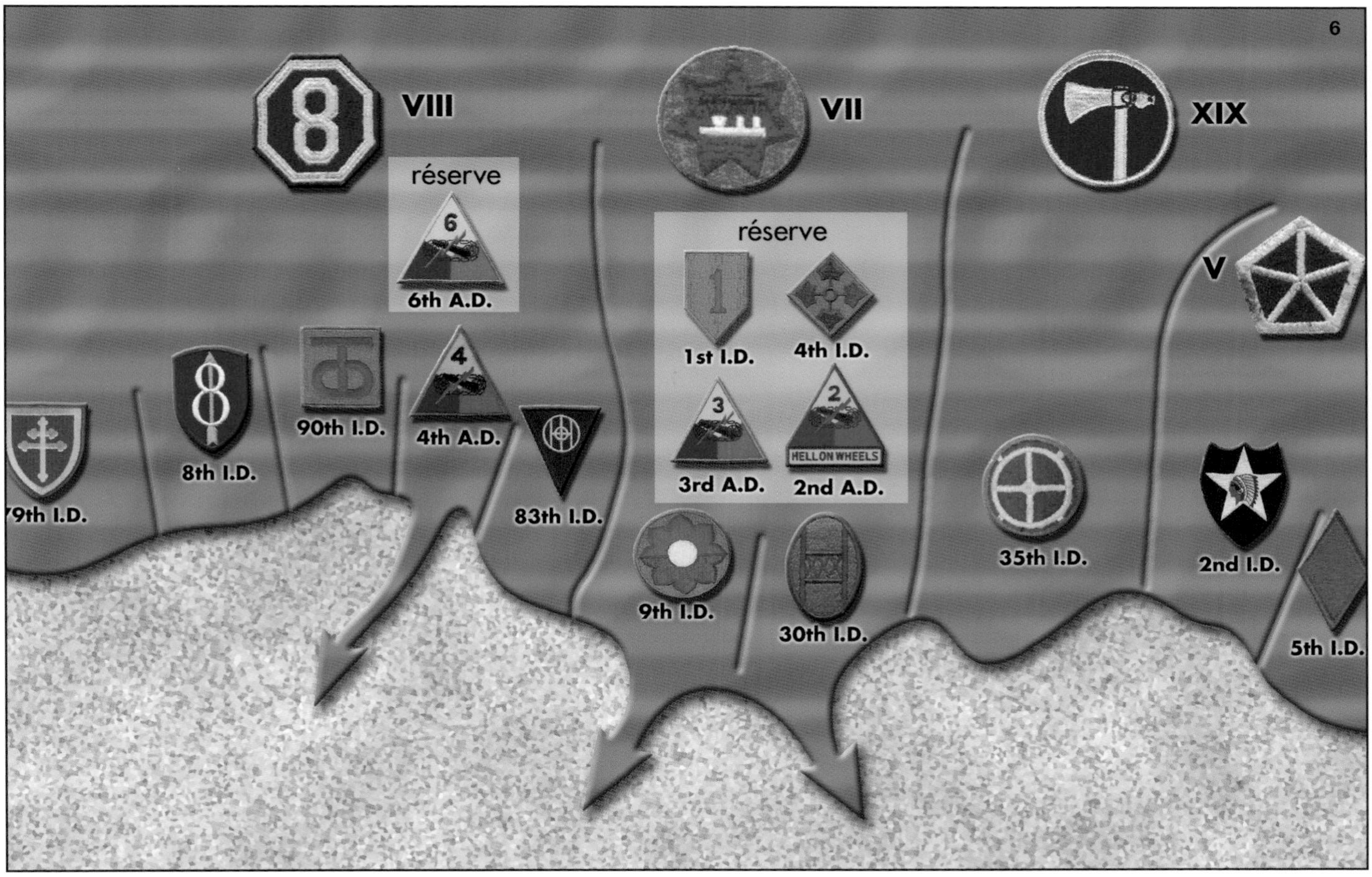

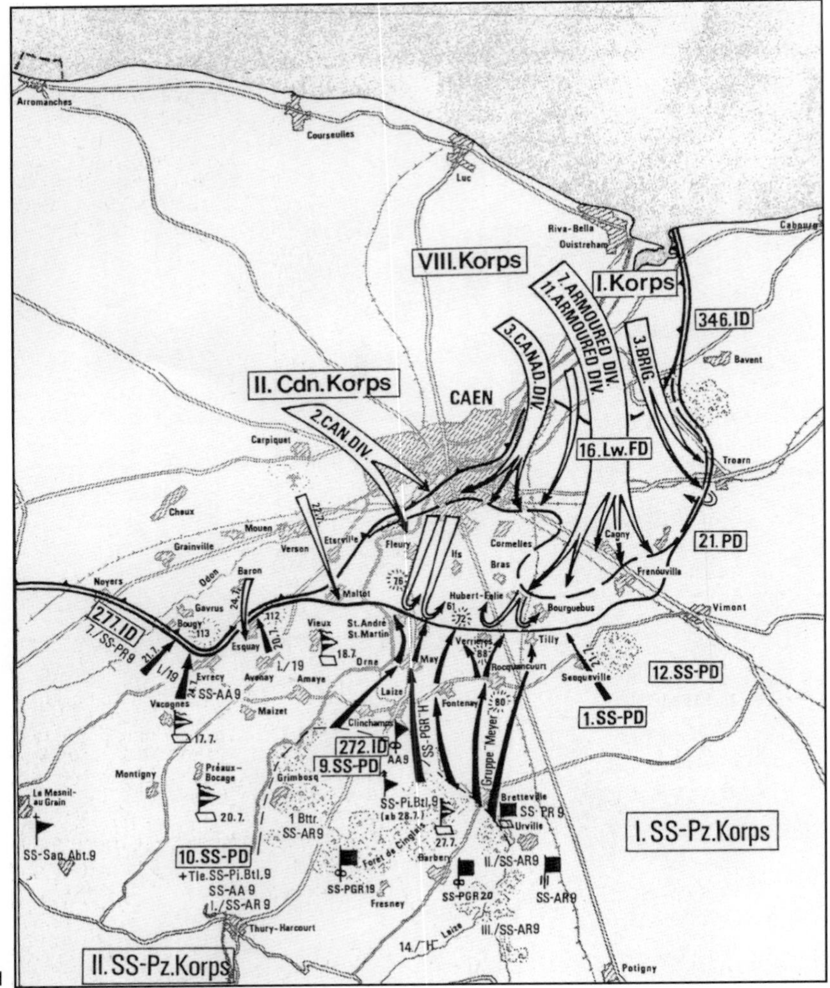

1. Operation Spring and the 9.SS-Panzer-Division counter attack in the 272. ID sector, July 25th till July 31st 1944. (H. Fürbringer/Heimdal.)

Spring (July 25th-31st)

Aln the aftermath of the heavy losses in tanks sustained during operation Goodwood, the VIII British Corps, exhausted, passes control of the Bourguébus ridge on to the II Canadian Corps (2nd ID, 3rd ID, 2nd Armoured Brigade) whose mission is to regain the initiative south of Caen. But on July 21st, the « Fusiliers de Mont Royal » are annihilated by a HJ Kampfgruppe around the Beauvoir and Torteval farms. Fifteen canadian tanks are lost, under heavy rains and thunderstorms. On the 22nd and 23rd, the onslaughs all end up in failure. The 3rd Canadian Division faces elements of the 1.SS-Pz.Div. and a Kampfgruppe of the HJ. The 2nd Canadian Division is up against the 272. ID and elements of the 9.SS-Pz.Div. and 10.SS-Pz.Div. A german counter attack fails on the 22nd due to Allies air superiority.

As to the west Operation Cobra gets underway, Operation Spring jumps off on July 25th at 03.00 hours east of the Orne river. The plan calls for a rush to the May sur Orne/Verrières/Tilly la Campagne line and the Fontenay le Marmion/Hill 122 line (7th Armoured Division). The objectives also include an advance southward and to Cintheaux (Guards Armoured Division). Following a devastating artillery barrage and under an artificial moonlit sky created by powerful searchlights, the canadian corps moves up one kilometer. To the east of the Falaise road (Heighway RN 158), the 9th Brigade, 3rd Division suffers heavy casualties to elements of the Leibstandarte. The artificial moonlight gives away the figures of advancing Canadians to the German defenders. The NNSH (North Nova Scotia Highlanders) loses 140 men. To the west of the RN 158 heighway, the 2nd Division engages its 4th Brigade towards Rocquancourt and its 5th Brigade to May sur Orne. In this sector, numerous iron mines facilitate German counterattacks to the Canadians rear. Furthermore, the canadian advance has been observed by the Germans from Hill 112 west of the Orne river who zero in their artillery and Nebelwerfer. Elements of the Hohenstaufen counter attack towards Rocquancourt and Tilly, at 13.05 hours with a Kampfgruppe and heavy tanks (under Otto Meyer's command, leading a tank Regiment), III./20, an Engineer company and a Flak Battery. Another KG (Zollhöfer), with the remnants of the division attacks from the west towards May, Saint Mar-

3. Later on, an ammunition truck has been hit by artillery shell. Soldiers run for cover behind a vehicle of the heavy weapons carrier regiment (Inns of Court, C Squadron) from the 1st Corps as the truck explodes. (IWM.)

4. A canadian Churchill tank in Vaucelles, southern part of Caen, on the way to the front. Period color photo. (PAC.)

2. July 26th in the British 1st Corps sector. Air cover above a convoy ; A RAF Typhoon fighter bomber taking off from an airfield as the convoy heads for the front. During the entire battle of Normandy, Allies air superiority has been complete. (IWM.)

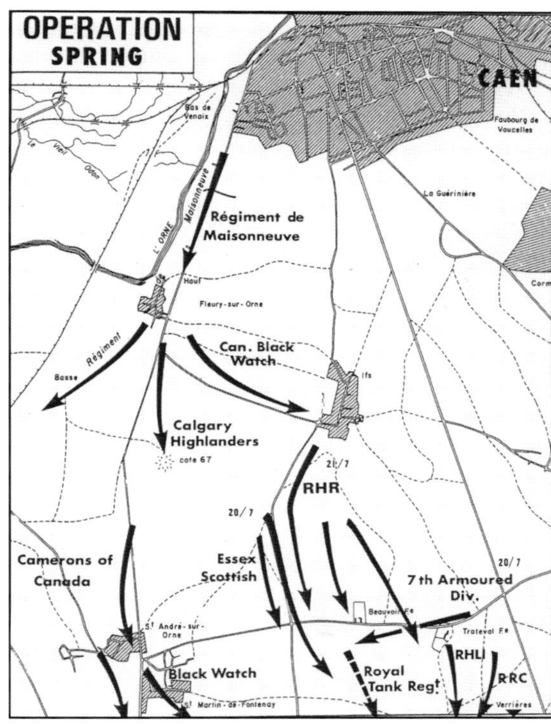

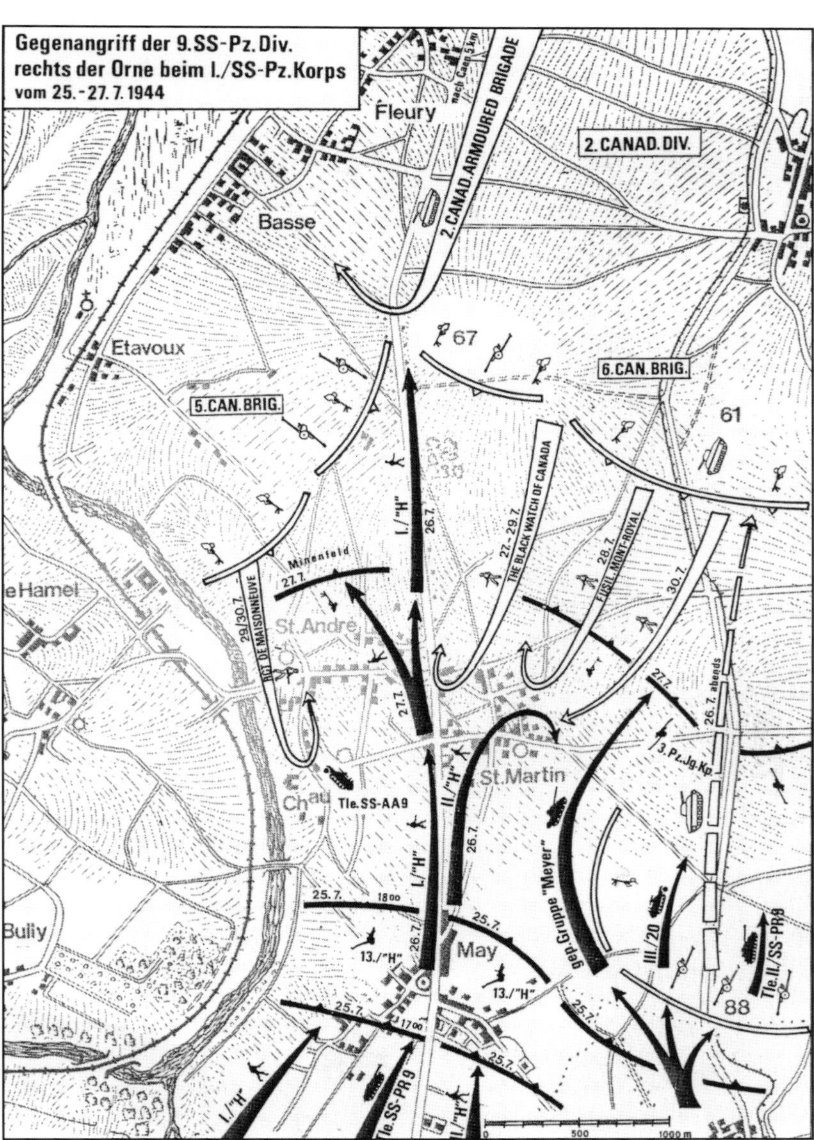

tin and Saint André. May (to the west) and Tilly (east) are out of reach.

The Hohenstaufen resumes the attack. On the 26th. KG Zollhöfer seizes Saint Martin and Saint André after four hours of furious engagements. On the right flank, the panzers of KG Meyer are under attack by Typhoons and Hill 88 is only taken by nighfall. On the second day of the counterattack, the Germans have recovered most of the ground lost to the Canadians, closing on Fleury and Caen. The Canadians suffer 1 500 casualties, with 307 for the Black Watch alone. Units of the 2nd Canadian Infantry Division are progressively pulled back towards Fleury and Ifs for refitting with unexperienced soldiers. The Canadians shall repeatedly fail in front of May sur Orne, suffering horrendous casualties to the Hohenstaufen, from August 1st until 5th. They will have to wait for Operation Totalize on August 8th dropping 3 500 tons of bombs on the german positions to finally take May and Tilly from the 85.ID, the Hohenstaufen having by then moved to another area.

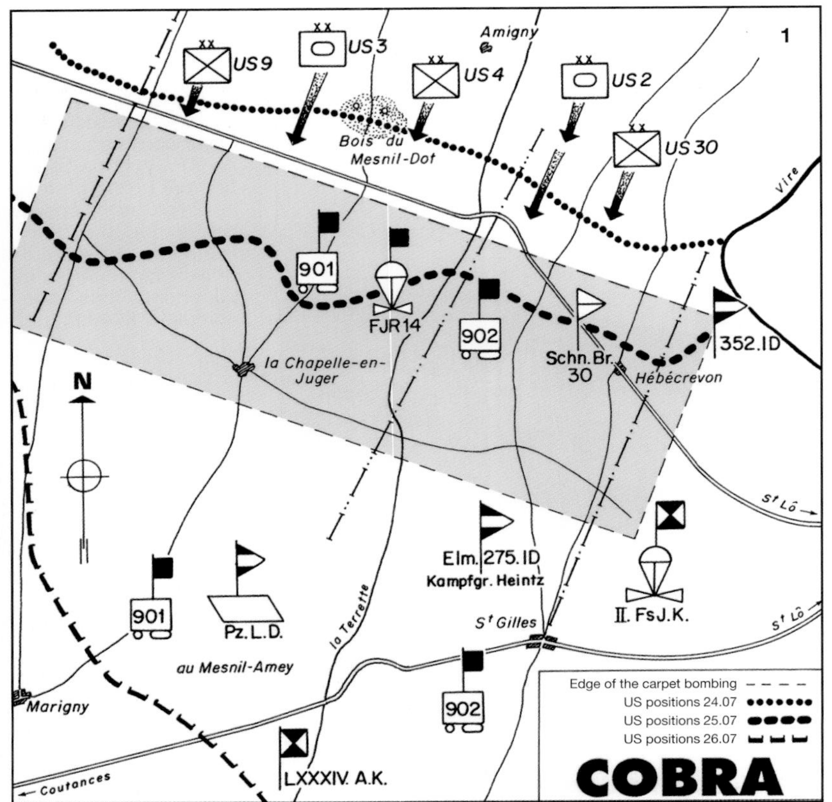

Cobra – the carpet bombing (July 24-26)

July 24th – Bombardment time is set for 13.00 hours. About 1 600 bombers take off from England (Six Fighter-Bombers Groups of the IX TAC and three bomber divisions of the 8th Air Force). Major General Collins has ordered the front lines of 9th and 30th division to make a quick 1 200 yards withdrawal in order to avoid any friendly bombardments. Unfortunately, visibility is poor in England and Air Chief Marshall Leigh-Mallory decides to postpone the attack. But all Groups cannot be reached and some bombardments take place in very bad conditions, resulting in the killing of 25 men and the wounding of 131st GIs in the 30th Division. Some procedure failures are to be blamed. The surprise effect is lost but it now matters not to lose momentum and give the Germans time to recover. Oddly enough, the Germans regard this « snafu » bombardment as « the real thing » and do not pull back. Bradley makes up his mind : Cobra will be in full effect on july 25th at 11.00 hours.

July 25th – 09.00 hours ; 1 500 B-17 and B-27 bombers reach their target and drop 3 300 tons of bomb upon the area to be saturated. Again, the american lines suffer huge casualties, (111 killed and 490 wounded). Lieutenant General Leslie McNair is among the dead, but combat fatigue brings the total losses on the american side for those 2 days to 814 casualties). Losses on the german side are horrendous. The Panzer-Lehr Division loses half his strength and can only account for 7 panzers out of 40 in working order. The attacking american corps faces isolated german resistance. An entire battalion of 8th IR, 4th ID is held up by two panzers and an handful grenadiers. The 8th IR only reaches la Chapelle en Juger by night fall. Major General Eddy faces unexpected resistance. He is reluctant to fully engage his 9th ID. After Goodwood's bitter failure, is this new large scale attack about to stall ?

July 26th – The german high command is short of reserves. There is no one to back those isolated groups even though the Panzer Lehr tries to fix its dismantled panzers. The PLD can rely on 14 tanks, and 14 more are being repaired. In the early hours of July 26th, the situation does not look much clearer for the Americans who gain very little ground. But the very last german resisting points collapse. To the east, on the left flank, the 30th ID rushes on, cutting the Coutances- Saint Lô road in the afternoon and closing on at nightfall the Canisy-Saint Lô heighway.The 30th ID CO Major General Hobbs is overjoyed. With all the good news, Major General Collins must decide on how to engage his armored forces. The CCB, 3rd Armored Division takes the right hand flank (west), while CCA, 2nd Armored Division rushes left (east). It reaches Canisy. Further west, VIII Corps is also attacking. General von Choltitz in charge of this sector of the german front, orders his troops on the left flank to pull back towards Coutances.

1. The area covered by the Cobra carpet bombing. The 9th ID and the tanks of the 3rd AD overrun the sector held by Regiment 901 of the Panzer-Lehr and FJR 14. The 9th ID lets the 4th drive through its lines. Objective ; Marigny. The 30th ID and the 2nd AD (hell on wheels) overun the Regiment 902, PLD, Schnele Brigade and KG Heintz sectors. Objective ; Saint Gille (Heimdal)

2. 9.00 hours, july 25th 1944. 1 500 B-17 and B-27 bombers reach their objectives and drop 3 300 tons of bombs on an area between Montreuil sur Lozon and Hébécrevon. Its hell from the sky. American lines suffer heavy casualties, 111 KIAs and 490 WIAs, almost the size of a battalion. This picture shows medics pulling out GIs from the dirt and rubbles of the explosions.

3. This Panther tank of the Panzer-Lehr Division weighting 45 tons has been tossed over inside a bomb crater. (Coll. Heimdal)

Opposite : in the aternoon of July 26th, tanks of CCB 3rd AD finally push to Marigny. Here are 2 Stuart light tanks of B Company 33rd Armored regiment. The one in the foreground is equipped with the « hedgecutter » device. (DAVA)

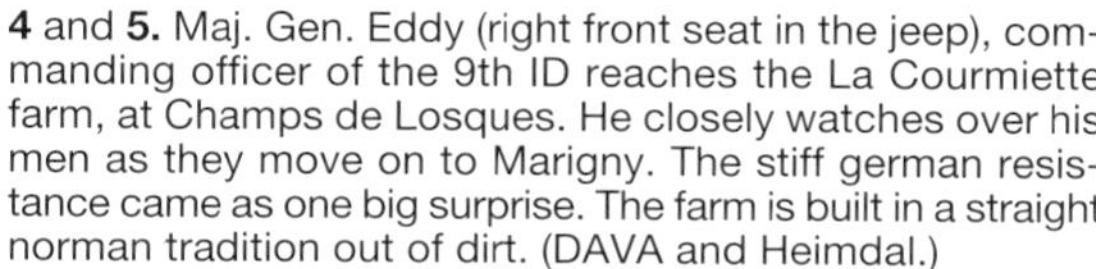

4 and **5.** Maj. Gen. Eddy (right front seat in the jeep), commanding officer of the 9th ID reaches the La Courmiette farm, at Champs de Losques. He closely watches over his men as they move on to Marigny. The stiff german resistance came as one big surprise. The farm is built in a straight norman tradition out of dirt. (DAVA and Heimdal.)

6. German paratroopers of the 5. Fallschirmjaeger-Division, most of them still wearing helmets are taken to the rear as Prisonners of War. They walk by a heavy armored truck from their own unit, with a WL plate. (Coll. Heimdal.)

7. Riflemen of the 30th ID walk through a torn Hébécrevon, a village they liberated in the evening of July 25th. Located on the Saint Lô-Périers road, the hamlet stood right under the bombing carpet. (Coll. Heimdal.)

8. Saint Gilles is one major important objective on the Saint Lô/ Coutances road, south of the bombing carpet area (see map). Coming from the north right before the intersection with that major heighway, a Sherman tank from the 2nd Armored Division (Hell on wheels) drives by a split Panzer IV from the 5th company, (II./130) PLD. The upper part has been blown away to the side. (Coll. Heimdal.)

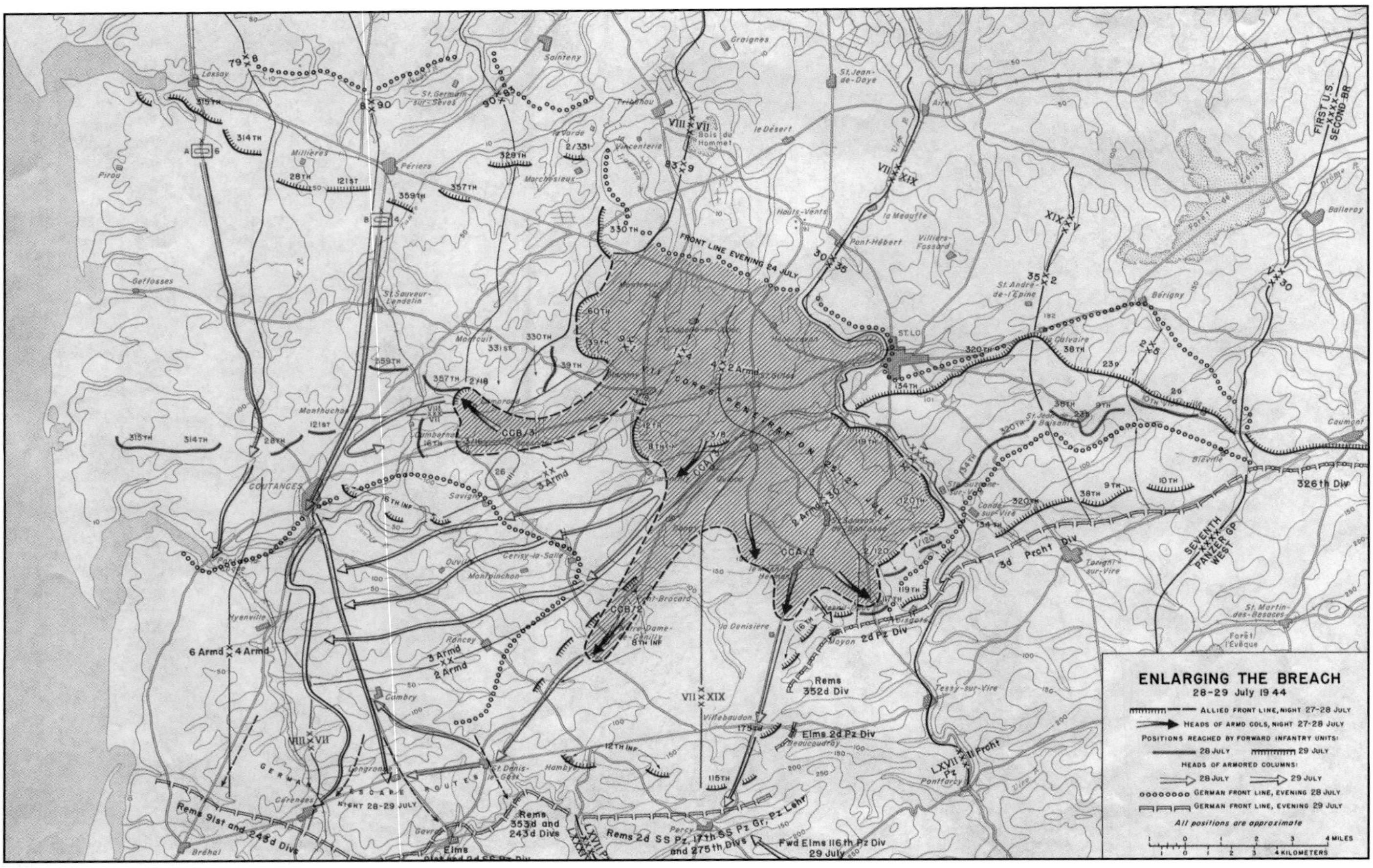

1

2

Cobra, the follow up (July 27-31)

The extension of the breakthrough quickly follows on July 27th. To the east, the 2nd Armored division moves up rapidly in front of desintegrating ennemies, and expands its lines in a widening movement, beyond Le Mesnil-Herman and all the way to Mesnil-Opac thanks to its CCA, then Pont-Brocard with CCB. On the western side, the extension also grows rapidly. CCB, 3rd Armored Division, holds the northen edge of the encirclement and tries to block the german withdrawal of the « Das Reich » and the « Götz », both establishing new lines of resistance to the north and east of what is to become the « Roncey pocket ». On this day, close to Neufbourg, on the road east of Coutances, SS-Uscha. Barkmann with his Panther tank of the « Das reich » knocks out 9 Sherman tanks and many vehicles within a few minutes.

On July 28th, the american offensive gets unexpected results. South east of Coutances, the 2nd Armored Division reaches Saint-Denis-le-Gast, closing the southern side of the Roncey pocket. To the north west, the 90th Inf. Div. has taken Lessay and Périers the previous night, paving the way for two brand new divisions, the 6th Armored Division only 4 kilometers away from Coutances, and the 4th Armored division coming from Saint Sauveur Lendelin and entering Coutances at sunset. On July 29th, the Americans outspeed the Germans who try to establish a new line of resistance south of Coutances (see map). The 4th AD rushes through Coutances while the Roncey pockets now holds at least 5 German divisions. The Germans try to break away during the night. Many will succeed and many will not make it : 2 500 KIA, 5 000 prisonners, 539 vehicles including over 100 tanks and 150 armored vehicles.

1. Broadening the american breakthrough of July 28th and 29th. This offensive is a threat to the rear of the german units positionned along the coast. They are forced to pull back. Two armored divisions to the west are hot on their heels, the 6th and 4th, entering Coutances as early as july 28th. But the 2nd Armored Division leads an outflanking attack and traps many german divisions in the Roncey pocket. The Germans retreat in the evening of july 29th on a defensive line Bréhal-Gavray-Percy. (Serv. Hist. Armée américaine)

2. Close behind the tanks of the 3rd Armored Division, riflemen storms Marigny late on July 26th. German units tactical signs on the telephone poll : Das Reich and above, KG Heintz. (DAVA/Heimdal.)

3. Canisy, July 27th. An M8 Armored car of a recon squadron (C squadron, 2nd Armored division) drives through a still burning town. Houses were set on fire by the artillery barrage the Americans called for prior to entering Canisy. (DAVA/Heimdal.)

4. In the beginning of the operation, the Marchésieux sector in front of the 83rd ID was held by the remnants of the 17. SS-Pz. Gren. Div. « Götz von Berlichingen ». On July 29th, a self propelled 105 mm HM2 Howitzer « Priest » drives by the burial of SS-Uscha. (sergeant) Joseph Richsfeld, born august 9th 1914 and KIA june 17th 1944 near saint Gilles. He belonged to the 9th battery, division artillery regiment, equipped with heavy 15 cm guns (Coll. Heimdal.)

5. Pont Brocard, July 29th. Riflemen of CCB, 2nd Armored division wait along a sunken lane to the west of Pont Brocard before cleaning up the place of isolated Germans who tried to escape the Roncey pocket. They are easy to identify thanks to their camo uniform designed to blend them into hedgerow country. (Coll Heimdal.)

6 and 7. Coutances, july 28th.Coming from Périers these US riflemen have reached the outskirts of town ; they're taking along a captured german NCO. (DAVA and E.G./Heimdal.)

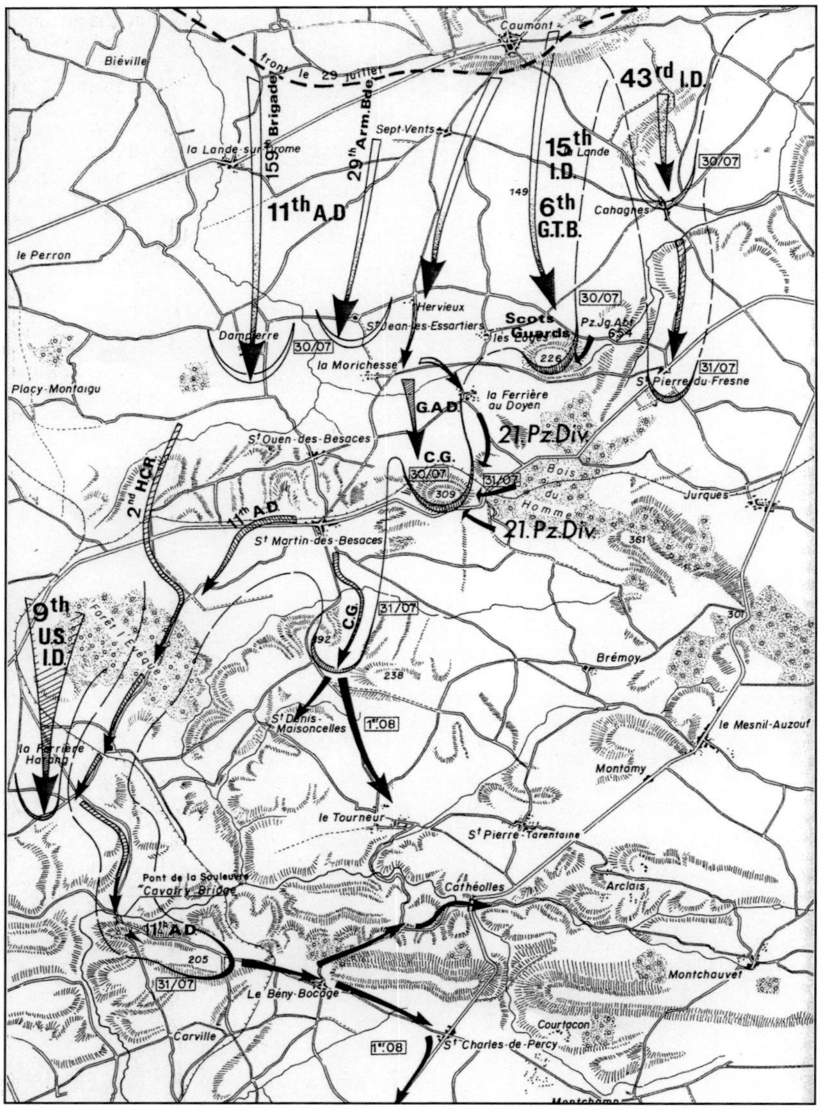

Bluecoat (July 30th-August 15th)

Thanks to Cobra, the German front is finally punctured to the west, under tremendous pressure from the First US Army. Montgomery follows the trade. Both operations Goodwood and Spring have come out as failures and the best opportunities for the Allies now stands on the left american flank of the breakthrough. From the Tilly sur Seules sector, XXX Corps, with its 50th ID, shall attack and head for Villers Bocage and Aunay sur Odon. The 50th ID shall be supported on its right flank by the 43rd ID and the 59th ID on the left with tanks of the 7th AD in reserve. The main objective is Hill 361 (also known as Mont Pinçon overlooking the entire region.)In the west, with the Caumont L'Eventé saliant as a base of departure, VIII Corps is to jump off with its 15th Scottish Division, supported by two armored divisions, the Guards Armoured Division and the 11th Armoured Division both supposed to make ground in a dense and rough Hedgerow country. Objective : Saint Martin des Besaces and Hill 309. They only face two german infantry divisions, the 326 ID in the west and 276. ID in the east.

The offensive starts on July 30th at 06.00 hours, with a three brigades front for each Corps. In the east, the 50th ID reaches Orbois while the 43rd ID takes Briquessard at noon. Cahagnes is seized by midnight. But in the west, tanks, chenillettes and half tracks get entangled in complicated minefields, creating gigantic traffic jams for over 30 000 vehicles in the Vire hedgerow country. Meanwhile, backed by 174 Churchill tanks of the 6th Guards Tank Brigade, the 15th Scottish Division reaches Hervieux and Hill 309 (to the north east of Saint Martin des Besaces). But at this point, it is hit hard by the counter attack led by the formidable Jagdpanther tanks of Panzerjaeger-Abteilung 654 in the vicinity of Hill 309, to the west of Bois du Homme. By dawn on the 31st, the remnants of 21. Panzer-Division, covered by the 65 tons Tiger II tanks of s.Panzer-Abteilung 503 also counter attack in the Bois du Homme area but fall under attack by 60 impressive Typhoon fighter-bombers which knock out 30 panzers and 54 armored vehicles.

1

1. Advance of VIII Corps with the 11th Armoured Division, the Guards Armoured Division (GAD), the 15th Scottish Division and the 6th Guards Tank Brigade, as well as the 43rd Division (XXX Corps) , from July 30th til August 1st 1944 (Heimdal)

2

2. July 30th, south of Caumont, Operation Bluecoat begins. Following a powerful artillery barrage and a violent air bombardment, tanks of the 4th Grenadiers Guards/ 6th Guards Brigade support the attack by the 15th Scottish Division.

3

3. July 31st, the advance continues. Saint Martin des Besaces main street - the village has just been liberated at noon by the 11th Armoured Division. (IWM.)

4. August 9th, Plessis-Grimoult sector, south of Mont-Pinçon, 7th Armoured Division. Coming across a column of prisonners, a Sexton from 59th AT. Regt. watches the road leading to Plessis-Grimoult. The weather is hot. Most of the artillerymen are bare chested and helmetless. (IWM.)

Further west, the 11th Armoured Division has broken through all the way to Saint Martin des Besaces taken at midday. Furthermore, as early as 10.30 hours, armored vehicles of the 2nd Household Cavalry have found an bridge intact over the Souleuvre river six kilometers to the south east of the village. This capture right at the connecting point of two german divisions (3.FJD in the west and 326.ID in the east) gives the tanks of the Guards Armoured Division a chance to sneak into the gap. On August 1st, the 21. Panzer-Division keeps on counter attacking under heavy shelling by artillery and fighter bombers that eventually bring it to a halt and a hastly withdrawal, with Tommies of the VIII Corps hot ont its tail. However, the 21.PD will not give Le Tourneur away to the 5th Armoured Brigade of the Guards until noon.

August 2nd, the 11th Armoured Division holds Le Bény Bocage, covering its approaches over two kilometers in depth. The previous night, its recon units have walked into Vire. But from the Caen southern sector, the Hohenstaufen rushes to the rescue (See Spring). Kampfgruppe Otto Meyer arrives at dawn and immediately goes into the attack on Montchauvet. Its panzers fight off the Guards tanks. More reinforcements come on the German side : Tiger I of the s.SS-Panzer-Abteilung 102 and the Frundsberg. This ends up in a stalemate ; the British no longer advance. The 7th Armoured Division fails to beat off the Frundsberg in front of Aunay sur Odon. The front line is once again static and British casualties raise in this area. The front line shall get on the move again once Panzergruppe Eberbach shall decide on the 3rd at 01.00 hours to shorten his lines and disengage panzer units to make them available for operation Lüttich (the Mortain offensive). Same story further east where the British seize without a fight Villers-Bocage (August 4th), Aunay sur Odon and Evrecy, then Hill 112 (August 5th), cross the Orne river at Grimbosq (August 6th) and close in on Falaise. But in this sector, the 11th Armoured Division, the Guards and the 15th Division are still stuck, losing some 40 tanks each day. 39 Sherman tanks are knocked out of action on August 4th near Chênedollé by Willy Fey's Tiger. The Germans will not pull out from there until August 15th, as part of a general withdrawal.

4

5

5. August 15th, the 11th Armoured Division in Vassy. Infantry follows the tanks breakthrough. A column of the KSLI (King's Shropshire Light Infantry) walks through Vassy on the way up to the front. (IWM)

The Pursuit (August 1st-6th)

Thanks to the Avranches breakthrough, another american army, Patton's Third, steps into Brittany on August 1st and rushes to the Val de Loire. Patton reaches Mayenne and Laval on August 6th. In the meantime, the First Army widens the Avranches breakthrough into a corridor and moves on Percy and Villedieu les Poêles on August 6th. CCA, 2nd Armored Division faces Vire. The 4th Infantry Division is in the Saint Pois sector. CCB, 3rd Armored Division has reached the Reffuveille area and the 30th Infantry Division arrives at Mortain on August 6th.

But Hitler has oredered a counter attack in Mortain, at the american corridor narrowest point, in order to take Avranches. The main objective is to completely cut off Patton's Third Army, severing its supply lines, and destroy it with the german divisions based in Brittany. Succesful in the USSR, this kind of plan is doomed to failure in the west because of the uncontested air superiority of the Allies. A german armored force is quickly assembled for this counter attack. The XLVII. (r.47) Panzer-Korps, with its 116. Panzer-Division, the 2. Panzer-Division, the 2.SS-Panzer-Division « Das Reich », the 1.SS-Panzer-Division « Leibstandarte » and one Kampfgruppe of the 17. SS-PanzerGrenadier-Division. This armored corps is made of only four divisions (some of them largely understrength beacause of heavy casualties sustained) when Hitler asked for seven. And the Allies air superiority has two main effects : The Germans movement of their armored forces to the front is delayed, and once on the line, these forces will be crushed by the destructive power of the fighter bombers before even reaching their line of departure. Was this plan suicidal ? Hitler thought he could rely on some aerial support to give his armor some air cover. One thousand fighter planes removed from the Reich air defense were dispersed before even reaching Normandy.

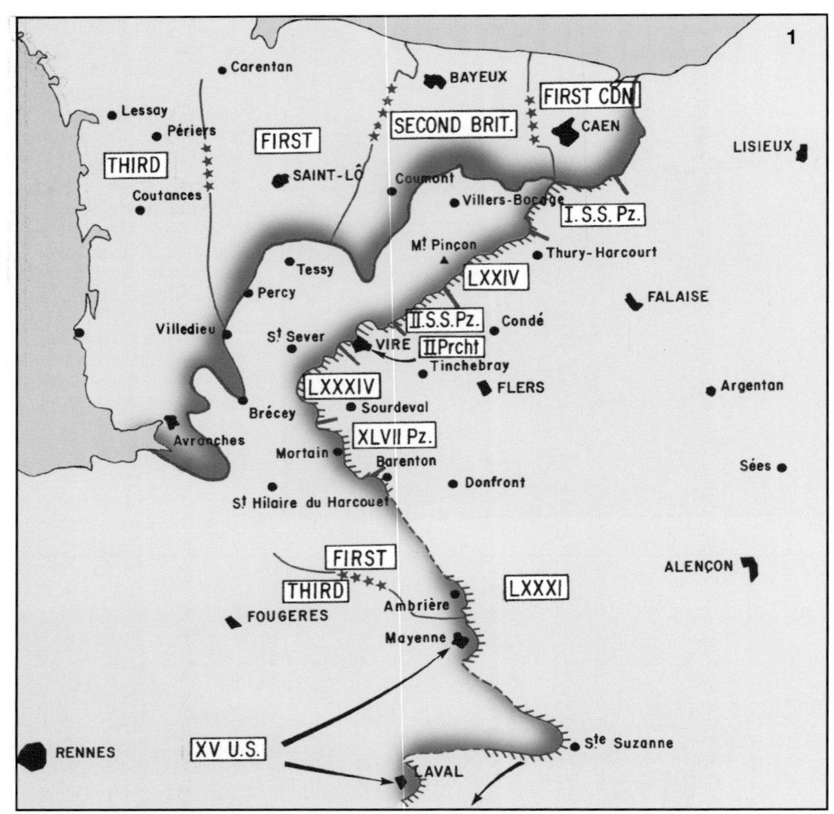

1. Here is a map showing the evolution on the Normandy front between August 1st and 6th, with Patton's advance on the side of Lt. Gen. Courtney Hodges First Army. These two armies fall under 12th Army Group high command, Lt Gen Bradley commanding. During these six days breakout,

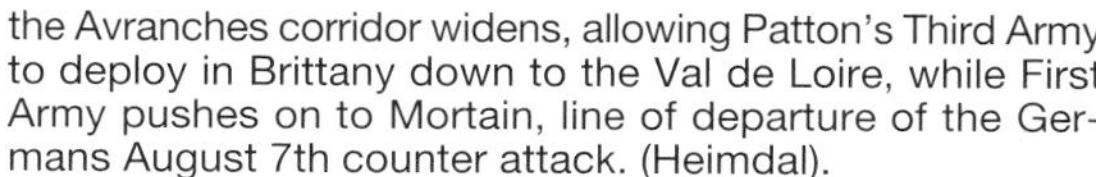

the Avranches corridor widens, allowing Patton's Third Army to deploy in Brittany down to the Val de Loire, while First Army pushes on to Mortain, line of departure of the Germans August 7th counter attack. (Heimdal).

2 and **3.** August 3rd, Tessy sur Vire. South of Saint Lô. This little town is a gateway to the Vire valley, very deep at this point. This picture was taken that very day at the Saint Lô (left) and Torigny (right) crossroads. These two roads are under the control of a small Stuart tank and a M10 Tank Destroyer. The place has remained unchanged. (Coll. Heimdal and E.G./Hdl.)

4 and **5.** On the american left flank, the german front south of Saint Lô holds until July 31st. The 2.Panzer-Division arrives in this area on July 29th and knocks out 29 american tanks. The division pulls back to Moyon on August 1st and Pont-Farcy where this picture was shot on the third. Visible is a wrecked Panzer IV from Panzer-Regiment 3, 2.PD. This tank was standing guard at the crossroad. The place has been modified with the reconstruction of the ruined house. (The new house in the center of the photo taken from a different angle, the panzer was sitting to the left, its rear towards the crossroad.) (Heimdal.)

6. Between Villedieu les Poêles and Mortain the going is fast. Here is a self propelled gun M7 firing at german units in Saint Pois on August 3rd, west of Périers en Beauficel and Sourdeval. (Coll. Heimdal).

7. Picture taken two days later in Saint Pois, August 5th, showing the outcome of the fighting. A Panther type A tank has been knocked out, and the tanker's body still lays in front of the wreckage. (Coll. Heimdal.)

8 and **9.** West of Sourdeval, a Sherman tank drives through an intact Périers en Beauficel. (Heimdal.)

10. August 4th in Villedieu les Poêles ; this GI of the 12th Infantry Regiment (4th ID) takes a break. (Coll. Heimdal.)

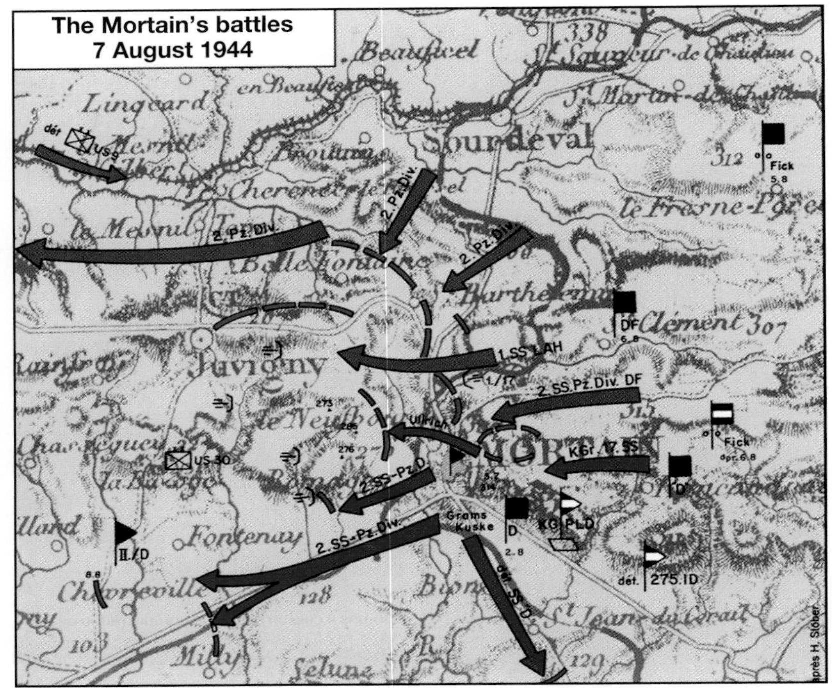

1

2

The Mortain offensive (August 7th-10th)

The german armored forces slowly move up to the front and on August 6th, Marshall von Kluge decides to speed up the pace and to launch operation Lüttich, the Mortain counter attack. Only 145 panzers (hardly the theorical full capacity of one sigle panzer division !) attack on August 7th at dawn, without waiting for all units to assemble. The 2. Pz-Div makes some progress in the northern edge of the front, about 8 kilometers deep to Mesnil Adelée while on the southern edge, the 2.SS-Panzer-Division advances 10 kilometers westward, reaching Fontenay and Milly. North of Mortain, around Hill 317, elements of the 120th Infantry Regiment (30th Division) are surrounded. The « Das Reich » has already covered one third of the distance between Mortain and Pontaubault. But the morning hazes soon vanish and from midday on, fighter bombers appear, pinning mercilessly the german armors before they can even get into a fight with the american tanks of the 3rd Armored division stationned in the area. A great number of Panzers are burning (about 60). The onslaught is broken. In the evening, Maj. Gen. Collins has two armored divisions and five infantry divisions available in his VII Corps thanks to quick reinforcements.

On the morrow August 8th, and in spite of the heavy casualties sustained, this desperate counter attack is renewed. The american forces are by then far superior. The german onslaught falters but the order will stand until August 10th, without any significant result.

On the 8th in the evening, Le Mans is liberated in a joint effort by the Third Army and the First Army on

3

4

5

its left flank. This city will be used as a line of departure for the attack on Alençon. The Americans are outflanking the german front in Normandy. On August 10th, the Canadians are at a mere 10 kilometers from Falaise. To the south, the Americans (XV corps, Third Army) are between Le Mans and Alençon heading north and fighting off a freshly arrived german division, the 9.Panzer-Division.

1. Combat in the Mortain sector (Heimdal.)

2. August 9th, officers of an american artillery unit have established an observation post to zero in their guns on Barenton, south east from Mortain. (Coll. Heimdal.)

3. The little town of Mortain will for a few days act as a pivotal point of the counter attack. On August 7th, the Americans set up an anti tank gun in expectation of the german onslaught. (Coll. Heimdal.)

4 and **5.** August 13th, after the fightings, american war correspondants stroll down the streets of Mortain evacuated by the Germans. The city is in ruins. A wrecked jeep and a half track have been pushed aside on the side walk. The place remains unchanged in spite of the reconstruction. (Heimdal)

6. After the failure of the german offensive, Americans check on german vehicles knocked out by fighter-bombers near the Mortain-Le Neufbourg railroad station. This station, visible in the background, sits in the valley at the bottom of the granite ridge where the city of Mortain has been built. The results of the fighter-bombers action are terrible. In the foreground is a vehicle from the 2. Pz-Div, recognizable because of the trident emblem on its side. Also visible is a Schwimmwagen, a jeep and a Kettenkrad. (Coll. Heimdal.)

7. The railroad station, no longer in use, still shows impacts of the fightings. (E.G. /Heimdal).

8. Further down the road, a half tracked vehicle and a Kettenkrad (tracked motorcycle). (Coll. Heimdal.)

9. Same vehicle seen from the opposite side, and the body of a soldier killed by « Jabos ». (Coll. /heimdal.)

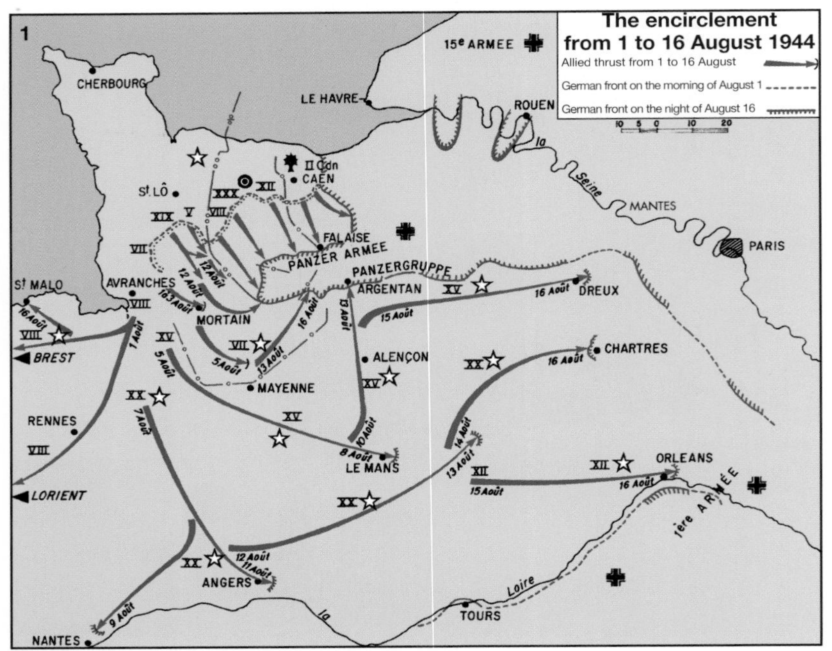

From Alençon to Argentan (August 12th-16th)

August 12th is one of the most decisive day in the battle of Normandy. Two armored divisions from the XV Corps (Major General Oliver's 5th Armored Division and Général Leclerc's own french 2nd DB on the left flank) seize Alençon and reach Argentan. Some american and french tanks of the 2nd DB even get into Argentan, only twenty three kilometers from Falaise. But the Canadians have not yet reach Falaise and Generals Montgomery and Bradley fear friendly fire incidents between Americans and their canadian friends at the closing of the pocket where most of the german army in Normandy could be trapped. Lt. Gen. Bradley orders Patton to make a stand in front of Argentan. A wonderful opportunity has been wasted. On August 13th, the German High Command begins to evacuate its forces, starting with the ever important rear units and their logistics capabilities. So it is on this very day, the 12.SS-Panzer-Division « Hitlerjugend » (according from its chief of staff) has already moved back to the eastern part of Normandy 10 000 men, keeping in line a tactical group of 1 500 men, 20 tanks and sixteen 88 mm guns. Same procedure goes for other units such as the 17.SS-Panzergrenadier-Division whose main body has already retired to the Lorraine area for refitting. On August 14th,General Eberbach, commanding officer of the 5. Panzer-Armee, request an order to pull back to avoid complete destruction. In the meantime, Bradley thinks the Germans have made good their escape and decides to run for the Seine river. But on August 15th, orders change and the Canadians head for Trun while the Americans keep moving eastward. On August 16th, XV Corps is in Dreux, XX Corps in Chartres and XII Corps in Orléans. The advance is spectacular but the Falaise-Argentan pocket has still not been closed when Hitler orders a general withdrawal at 11.53 hours.

Soldiers of the 39th Infantry Regiment (9th infantry Division) set up a bazooka in the Andaines forest (north west of Alençon) on August 15th. They carry their division insignia on their helmet and sleeve. This division is fighting between La ferté-Macé and Rânes. (Coll. Heimdal.)

As a result, between August 13th and 18th, 55 000 men, accounting for 40% of the troops threatened to be surrounded have pulled back. Bradley is right when he asseses that the bulk of the german army has made good their escape.

Finally, four days behind schedule, the closing of the falaise pocket occurs. Montgomery learns of Hitler's withdrawal general order and decides to get it over with, pushing his forces towards Trun in Canadian hands.

9th ID

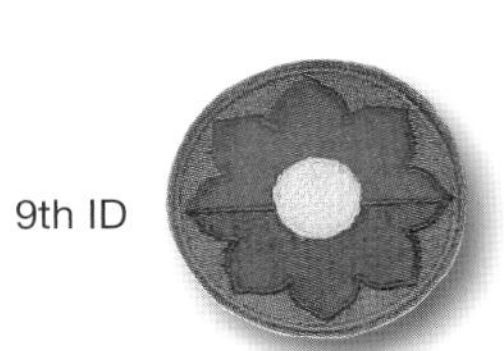

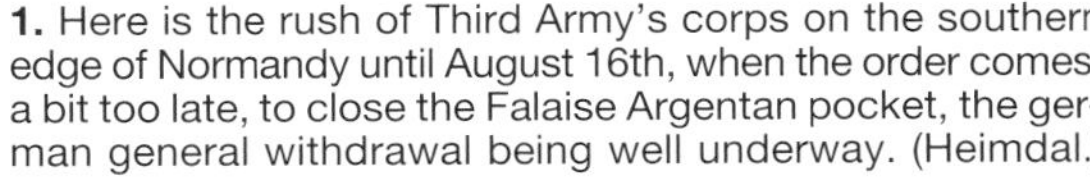

1. Here is the rush of Third Army's corps on the southern edge of Normandy until August 16th, when the order comes, a bit too late, to close the Falaise Argentan pocket, the german general withdrawal being well underway. (Heimdal.)

2 and **3.** North east of Sourdeval, on August 13th and east of Vengeons. The american advance is quick to the south when east of Mortain, the going slows down agains stubborn german resistance in this sector. Here are riflemen of the 28th ID walking through the little village of la Haute Barre. (DAVA and H. de Prat/Heimdal).

4. Pfc Louis L. Hesse takes a short break at the Tinchebray, Domfront and Lonlay crossroads next to road signs left out by the Germans on August 16th. (DAVA/Coll. Heimdal.)

5. Inside Lonlay, the going gets tough for the american tanks. A few days earlier, a picture of the same spot showed vehicles of 116. Panzer-Division ready to counter attack. In the background is the steeple of the abbey. (Col. Heimdal.)

6. German Prisoners of War leaving Domfront on August 14th on the Mortain road. No more counter offensive for these men. (NA/Coll./Heimdal.)

7. Domfront, Augst 14th : German POWs and american Gis of the 3nd Armored Division with camoed uniforms. (NA/Coll. Heimdal.)

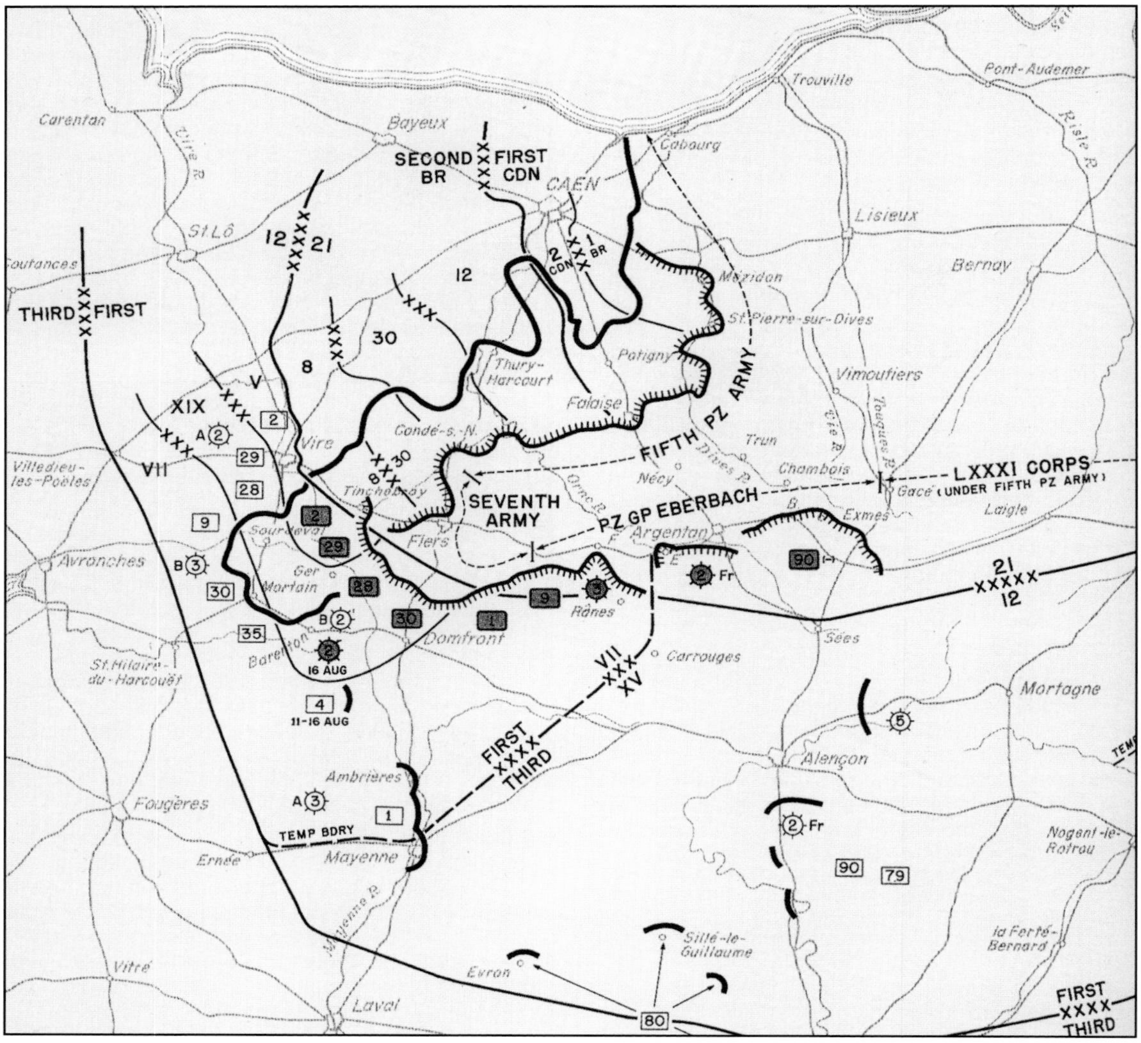

1. Evolution of the front line between August 12th (straight line) and August 16th (dotted line). During this period, the american army has moved up to Argentan and then come to a halt, while the Germans pulled back in the west and defended the northern edge of the front against British-Canadian pressure.

2. This picture was taken at Ecouché (west of Argentan) around August 16th. It shows, on the left, Colonel Warabiot, commanding officer of 501st RCC, 2nd French DB, assessing the situation with his officers. (IWM.)

Tractable (August 14th-16th)

Monday August 14th. In the south, the situation gets somewhat clearer for the Germans as the front line quiets down, with the american's axis of attack under Patton's orders to Haislip moving towards the Seine river. Montgomery also believes thats the bulk of the german forces have withdrawn. It is not yet the case even if the general withdrawal is well underway, some units being still engaged in the Flers sector. In the northern part of the saliant where german units are still pulling back, canadian divisions (2nd and 3rd Canadian Infantry Divisions, 4th Canadian Armoured Division as well as the Poles of the First Polish Armoured Division, all under First Canadian Army authority), get ready to move to the attack in the early hours of the day. Following an artillery barrage at 11.37 hours, the canadian tanks move up at 11.42 hours in a great state of confusion due to smoke and dust. The canadian corps makes good progress but smart delaying actions by the Germans slow them down. Falaise is still five kilometers away. The town is the corps main objective of the day according Montgomery's order. Further east, the second British Army makes movement towards Trun.

Tuesday August 15th, orders and counter orders delay the encirclement. Montgomery and Bradley hold an conference. Montgomery orders the American XV Corps to a defensive line south of Argentan while his own troops advance towards Falaise. The Canadians try to move up but sustain heavy casualties to Tiger tanks and elements of the Hitlerjugend Division (KG HJ).

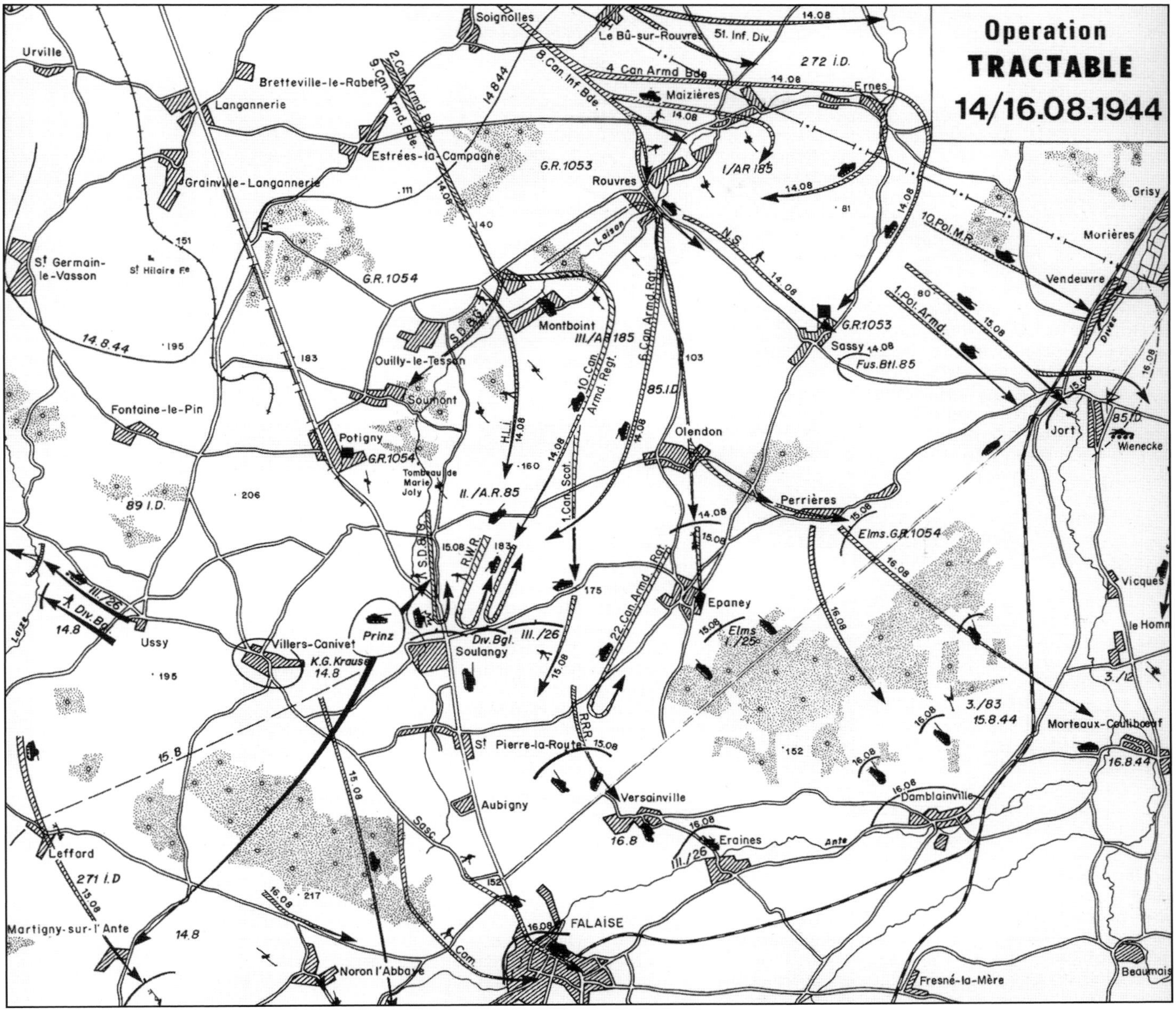

Operation TRACTABLE 14/16.08.1944

3

Wednesday Audust 16th. The german evacuation of the saliant continues. Between August 13th and 18th, 55 000 men, or a good 40% of all german forces on the edge of being surrounded have withdrawn. But at 15.00 hours, Montgomery releases the order to XVth Army Corps (american) to start moving. In the meantime, north of Falaise, General Simonds (commanding officer IInd canadian Corps) orders the link up with the Americans. At 15.00 hours, the 2nd Canadian Infantry Division launches an attack on Falaise. The Saskatchewans enter town at 17.30 hours, stubbornly defended by elements of the HJ. The battle will rage until the next day, 03.00 hours.

3. Map of operation Tractable and the liberation of Falaise.

4. A column of Sherman tanks of the 10th Brigade, 1st Polish Armoured Division moving up for operation Tractable. The marking « PL » for Poland is clearly visible. (IWM.)

1

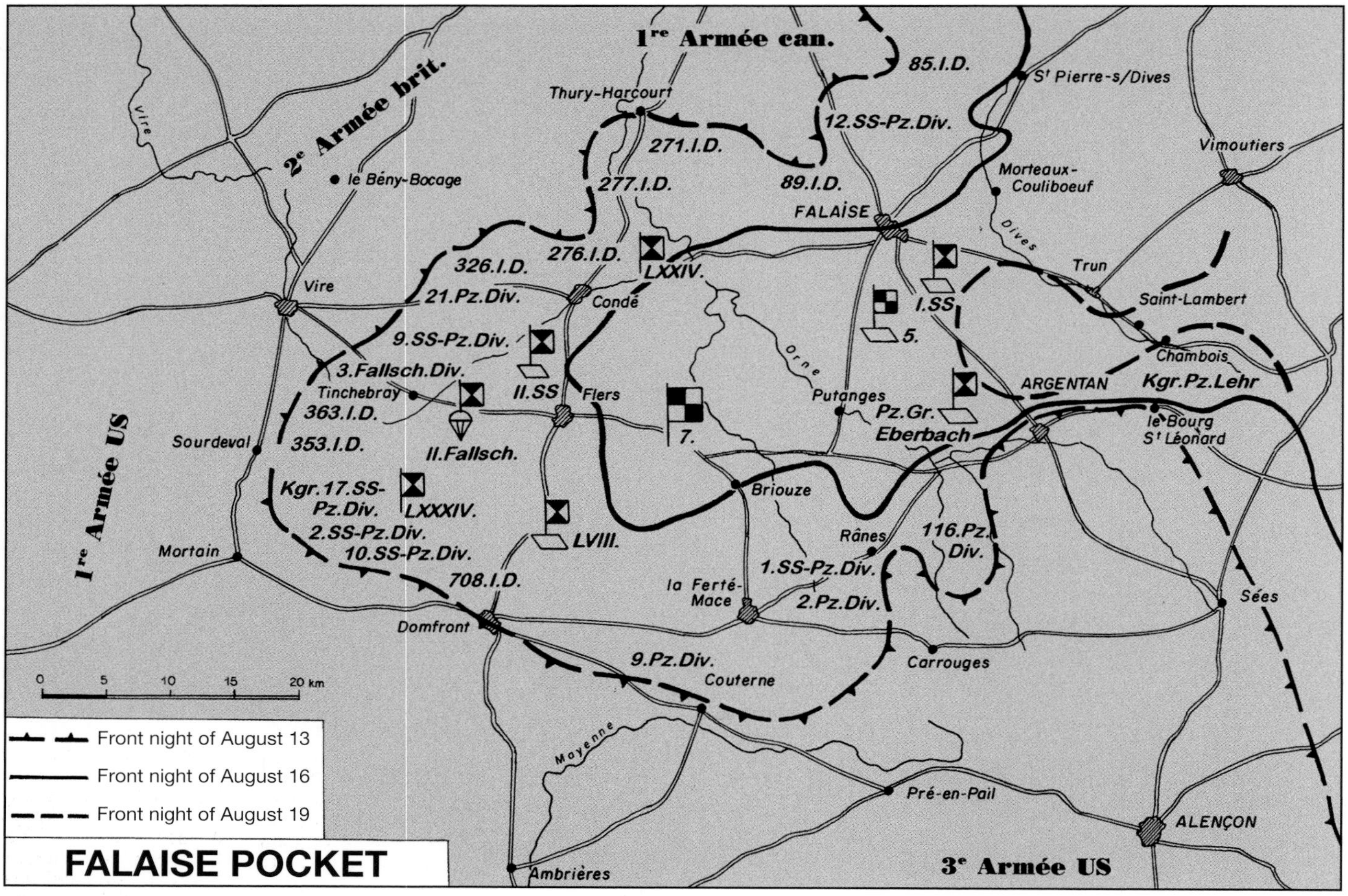

2

1. This map shows the successive withdrawals of the german troops inside the saliant. On August 17th, they pull back behind a major obstacle, the Orne valley, with Putanges as an important crossing point. This operation is a tremendous success achieved under dramatic conditions. Falaise falls under pressure, but Argentan still holds. (H. Fürbringer/Heimdal.)

2. Putanges has been an essential passage point above the river Orne on August 17th. This picture shot three days later shows a British Sherman tank of the 11th Armoured Division crossing the Orne on a Bailey bridge built upon the wrecked arches of the former bridge destroyed by the Germans. (IWM.)

Sealing of the pocket (August 17th – 18th)

Thursday August 17th, 06.30 in the morning. Under torrential rains, Major General Leonard T Gerow (Vth Corps) arrives in Alençon to launch the american offensive, take Argentan, and link up with the Canadians on a Chambois-Trun line. He has received

4

3

5

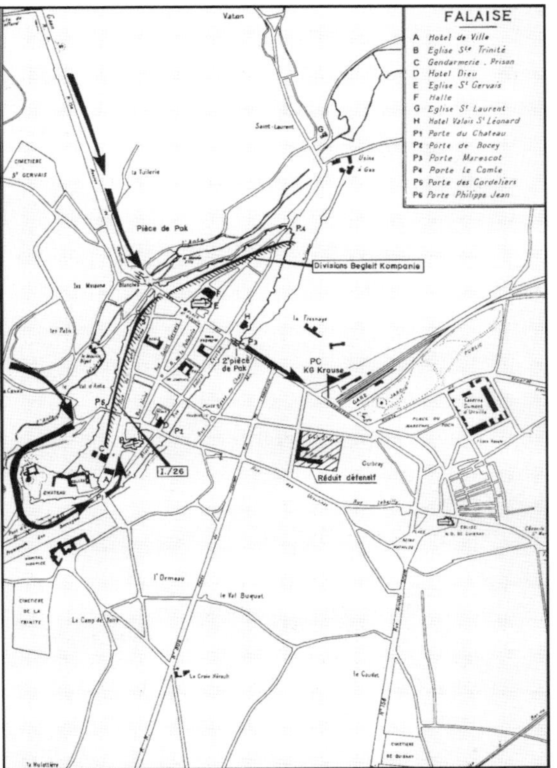

orders to take command of the XVth Corps divisions as this corps is now attached to First Army on the rush to the Seine river and Paris. The previous night, the german saliant still measured over 40 kilometers in length, with every inch covered by the Allies artillery. But overnight a withdrawal has been accomplished behind the Orne river and turned out « a remarkable success » (according to Martin Blumenson). The main crossing point has been Putanges. But as the withdrawal succesfully occurs, the main threat to the Germans is now in the north, in the Falaise sector. The last fights for the city are underway. At 03.00 hours, the Saskatchewans have reached the railroad crossing on the road to Trun, while fighting still goes on on the western part of the city. The Camerons arrive at dawn Place Trinité and reach the City Hall at 07.30. The Camerons make it to Saint Clair at 12.30 hours, to the south of the city, while isolated pockets of resistance, mostly Hitlerjugend's, still hold and for the rest of the day in the Ecole Supérieure de Jeunes filles high school area. More Hitlerjugend elements still hold strong at the north east of the city around Damblainville. However in the east, from the Jort bridgehead, elements of the 2st Polish Armoured Division close in on Trun, facing KG Luck. This is where the main threat comes from for the Germans. In Falaise, the lock is open but the Canadians only make litttle progress. It is within the Trun area that the main attempt for an Allied breakthrough is taking place, with the 1st Polish Armoured division as spearhead. This is where the end of the battle of Normandy is about to unfold. In the south, Argentan sector, the situation looks better on the german side, as the 116.Pz.Div holding the front has been reinforced the previous day by the II.SS-Panzer-Korps. Facing them are the 80th and 90th US Infantry Divisions and the French 2nd DB for the time appearing « quite passive », according to the 116.PD chief of staff. But the II.SS-PzK in turns start pulling back and Bourg Saint Leonard falls at 18.00 hours, a high ground objective.

Friday August 18th. Up north, the 4th Canadian Armoured Division closes in on Trun, with the 1st Polish Armoured Division aiming east of Chambois at a link up with the US 90th ID. In the Argentan sector, the situation deteriorates for the Germans even though the US 80th ID attacks on Argentan are being repelled. From Bourg Saint Leonard, the 90th ID now threatens Chambois. The exit door slowly closes down on the Germans.

3 and **4.** Falaise, August 17th 1944. Coming from the city center, canadian tanks (Sherbrooke Fusiliers) supported by Fusiliers de Mont Royal move up rue des Ursulines, parallel to rue des Prémontés, on the right hand side of the Ecole Supérieure block. They're seen here at the beginning of the street that has remained untouched. (PAC and G. Bernage)

5. August 18th, a canadian rifleman has just been decorated. He lights up a cigarette with some MP from the 2nd Canadian Infantry Division, near the fountain at the Falaise city center, Place Saint Gervais. The german road signs of 884 section of the Feldgendarmerie are still in place – color period picture. (PAC)

6. On this Falaise map appears the ancient city with its high walls. The August 16th fightings are beyond the grey line, and then the defensive strongpoint of the Ecole Supérieure, with the rue des Ursulines on the southern edge.

1. August 19th, the pocket is sealed. To the north, the Canadians are in Trun and close in on Saint Lambert. To the south, the Poles of Major Zgorzelski and the Americans of the 359th ID have linked up in Chambois now strongly held. GTL, 2nd French DB moves up to Mont Ormel, then backs up, still firing inside the pocket with its artillery. But the Germans still have an escape route from Saint Lambert to Moissy with one major obstacle ahead, the Poles dug in on Hill 262 (Boisjos), a spot they call « Maczuga » that closes the pocket. The Germans however succeed in sneaking north of Boisjos and Hill 262 around the obstacle. The pocket is not quite sealed. (Heimdal.)

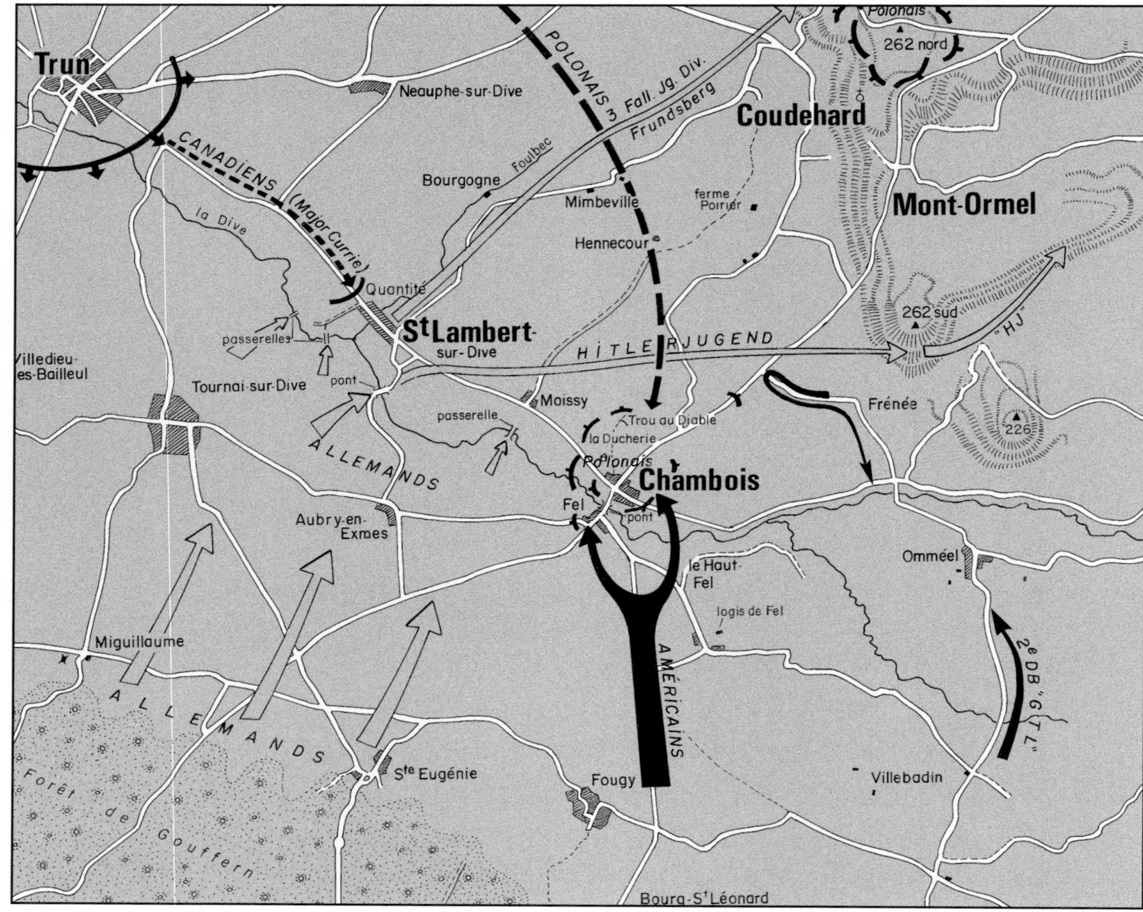

The link up (August 19th)

This is a decisive day for the Germans. All night long between the 18th and the 19th of August, the gap in the saliant has remained open and german troops have kept on retreating in good order. On this Saturday morning, the saliant measures about ten kilometers in length and twelve in width. Inside are the remnants of four panzer divisions (1.SS-Pz-Div., 10.SS-Pz.Div., 12.SS-Pz.Div., 2.Pz-Div. and 116. Pz. Div.), elements of the 2.SS-PZ.Div. and what is left of six infantry divisions (84.ID, 276.ID, 277.ID, 326.ID, 353.ID, 363.ID) as well as different units such as the parachutists of 3.FJD, and many tactical groups. All these units must from then on fight their way out before the trap closes in on them.They all have received order to regroup east of the Touques river. The crossing of the Dive river is scheduled for the following night.

But this is also a crucial time for the Allies who are able to close the salient and isolate the last retreating german units inside a pocket. The Canadians first follow their advance. In the early hours, a tactical group of the 4th Armoured Division comprising

2

3

4

2. Saint Lambert, August 19th. Canadian soldiers of B Company, Argyll and Sutherland Highlanders of Canada are about to walk into village. (PAC.)

3. German soldiers commanded by Hauptmann Rauch (seen here with googles on his cap) surrender to Major Currie (to the left pistol in hand) and to Colour Sergeant Major George Mitchell. Also noticeable on the left is a news cameraman filming. (PAC.)

4. Now and then picture taken in 1994. (Heimdal)

5. Symbolic photo commemorating the link up, this picture shot in Chambois by an American war correspondant on August 20th shows on the left lieutenant Wladyslaw Klaptocz of the 10th Polish Dragoon and Major Leonard C Dull who led the attack of his battalion on Fell and Chambois (including Captain Waters company). (US Army/Heimdal.)

6. Fifty years later, in 1994, Laughlin E Waters stands at the very same spot where he met Major Zgorgzelski as he explains to Georges Bernage.

7. This famous painting illustrates Typhoon fighter bombers attacking a retreating german tank columns through Saint Lambert sur Dive. The artist shows some panzers hit and burning in front of the Saint Lambert church with its steeple in the background. Two bridges over the Dive river are the Germans main getaway. It is inside this church that around 09.00 hours on August 20th SS. Oberführer Heinz Harmel (commanding officer 10.SS-Pz-Div. « Frundsberg ») urges his men to break away across the Dive. (IWM.)

8. This is the first bridge used by the Germans to cross one of the Dive two streams in Saint Lambert, looked over by George Bernage in 1994. (Heimdal.)

9. Picture shot with C. Plumey right after the fighting and showing two wrecked and overturned Panther. The house in the background is untouched. (Archives de guerre.)

B company, Argyll and Sutherland Highlanders of Canada and C Squadron, South Alberta Regiment, Major D.V. Currie commanding, reaches Saint Lambert. The same day late in the morning, the 1st Polish Armoured Division sends two tank regiments and a recon group to Chambois where they enter around 19.00 hours after salvage fighting. Around 19.45 hours, Major W. Zgorgzelski of 10th Polish Dragoons makes contact with 34 years old captain Laughlin E. Waters, commanding officer of G Company, 359th IR, 90th ID coming out of Bourg Saint Leonard under cover from tanks of GTL, 2nd French DB. The sealing of the pocket is achieved. But unlike the orders given by the 90th ID, GTL of 2nd French DB pulls back at nightfall beyond the Dive. As a result of this, the Chambois/Vimoutiers road is no longer cut between Saint Lambert and Mont Ormel. And with the slopes of Hill 262 running between the road and the French positions, this important axis is no longer covered by the 2nd DB artillery. This gap will prove essential the following days to favor the last german escapes.

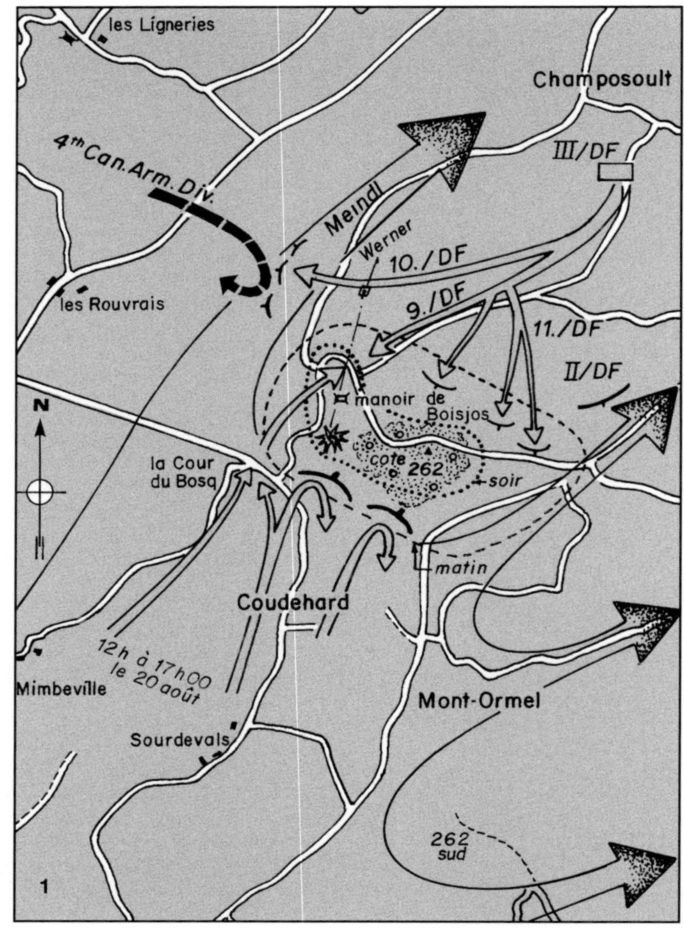

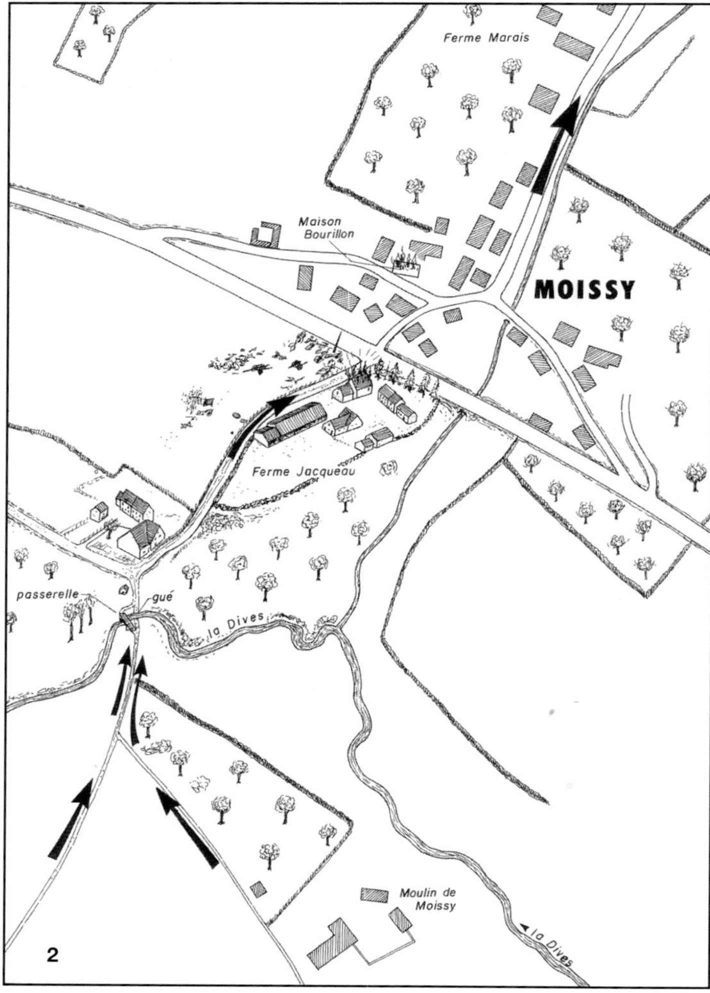

The breakthrough (August 20th-21st)

Sunday August 20th. The last preparations for the german breakthrough have been successfully carried out on the 19th. First elements of the II.Fallschirm-Korps (parachutists commanded by General Eugen Meindl) set off on the 19th around 22.00 hours, with strict orders to keep silent and avoid opening fire until dawn. The parachutists cross the river Dive a few kilometers north of Saint Lambert at the break of dawn and move on to the east. Then the 353.ID in turns crosses the river as rain starts to fall. When the morning haze lifts up, the Poles on Mont Ormel can see from the west dozens of long columns of german foot soldiers closing in on their positions. And behind those, the II.SS-Panzer-Korps launches its attack right on time at 08.00 hours sharp to open up the corridor. In the mean time, forward elements of the 3.FJD (parachutists) have reached Coudehard where they fall under a terrible artillery barrage. Around midday, Meindl and Hausser adjust their plans. Following a two hours artillery barrage, the Germans attack Mont Ormel and the ground held by the Poles (called Maczuga because of its club like shape) rapidly shrinks. The parachutists make contact with the forward elements of Regiment « Der Führer ». The road between Coudehard and Champosoult is open around 16.30 hours. Even tough covered by the Allied artillery that inflicts terrible losses to the fleeing Germans, it still represents an escape route to freedom. Another breakthrough, the one achieved by XXXVII. (r.47) Pz. Korps takes place in the south between Chambois and Saint Lambert, with the 1.SS-PZ.Div., the 2.Pz.Div. as early as 04.00 hours in the morning in horrible conditions, among dead soldiers and animals and wrecked vehicles. Also fleeing are KG HJ, 10.SS-Pz.Div. with SS-Oberführer Harmel boosting his men's morale inside the Saint Lambert church. On Maczuga, the Poles fire away without respite, under pressure of being overrun by the huge masses of fleeing german soldiers. The retreat of the IInd Parachutist Corps continues all night between the 20th and 21st, under pouring rain.To the south and bringing up the rear, the 116.ID has assembled north of the Goufern forest while the 80th US ID finally succeeds in entering Argentan. In the evening of August 20th, the retreat of II. Fallschirm-Korps and XXXVII. Panzer-Korps appears a complete success, the second phase of the plan seems obviously much more difficult to achieve ; the units trapped inside the pocket will have to fight their way out of the closing trap.

Ine the early hours of August 21st, Meindl gathers his men holding Coudehard, less than 3 500 men with only a few hundreds still in fighting condition. Around 07.00 hours they pass through the lines of the II.SS-Pz-Korps near Champosoult. Soldiers of the 2.SS-Pz.-Div. shall later tell how impressive the parachutists looked as they walked by singing. More groups cross the Dive later on that day but around noon, the Allies are holding the river banks and the pocket is definitely sealed. Some isolated elements still make it to the lines of the Das Reich that controls the exit but by 16.00 hours, no one else shows up. The Germans therefore have sucessfully evacuated a total of 100 000 men between August 13th and 21st. General Haislip's divisions were in front of Argentan on August 12th. Should have the order to attack been given, those 100 000 men, most of them elite troops, would have been trapped.

3

4

5

6

7

1. Maczuga, the Polish strongpoint, counter attacked from the rear and outflanked on all sides by the flow of fleeing german soldiers, perticularly through the south of Hill 262 and Mont Ormel, left unprotected. Meindl's parachutists escaped from the north. The shrinking defensive perimeter is clearly visible. (Heimdal)

2. The Dive river, about two meters deep, stood as a serious obstacle in the escape path of the Germans who will cross it mostly in Saint Lambert, after the fall of Trun and Chambois, and also at the Gué de Moissy. Besides the foot bridge, the ford this time of the year is useable. Hundreds of vehicle will use it. Lots of them have been destroyed by strafing, artillery shells or simply abandonned. (Heimdal)

3. Overall view showing the Jacqueau farm (looking south) at the exit of the Moissy ford. In front and to the left, the road from Trun and leading to Chambois, with Saint Lambert behind the photographer. Wrecked german vehicles litter the path. (IWM.)

4. The Jacqueau farm restored ; nothing remains of the intense fightings. (Fabrice Corbin)

5 and **6.** Before the last operations of the sealing of the pocket, until August 19th,the road from Chambois to Mont Ormel has been used for the german withdrawal. It will be momentarily cut off by the polish troops but will nevertheless allow the fleeing german troops to slip through until August 21st. The german vehicles destroyed by Allied air power and mostly by artillery fire litter both sides of the road. Todays landscape leaves no hint of the drama that took place here. (IWM and Fabrice Corbin)

7. August 21st 1944. The city of Argentan finally falls into american hands after fierce fighting by the 116. Panzer Division whose one of its Panther type A is here visible. The smoking ruined houses are still dominated by the saint Germain church. (IWM.)

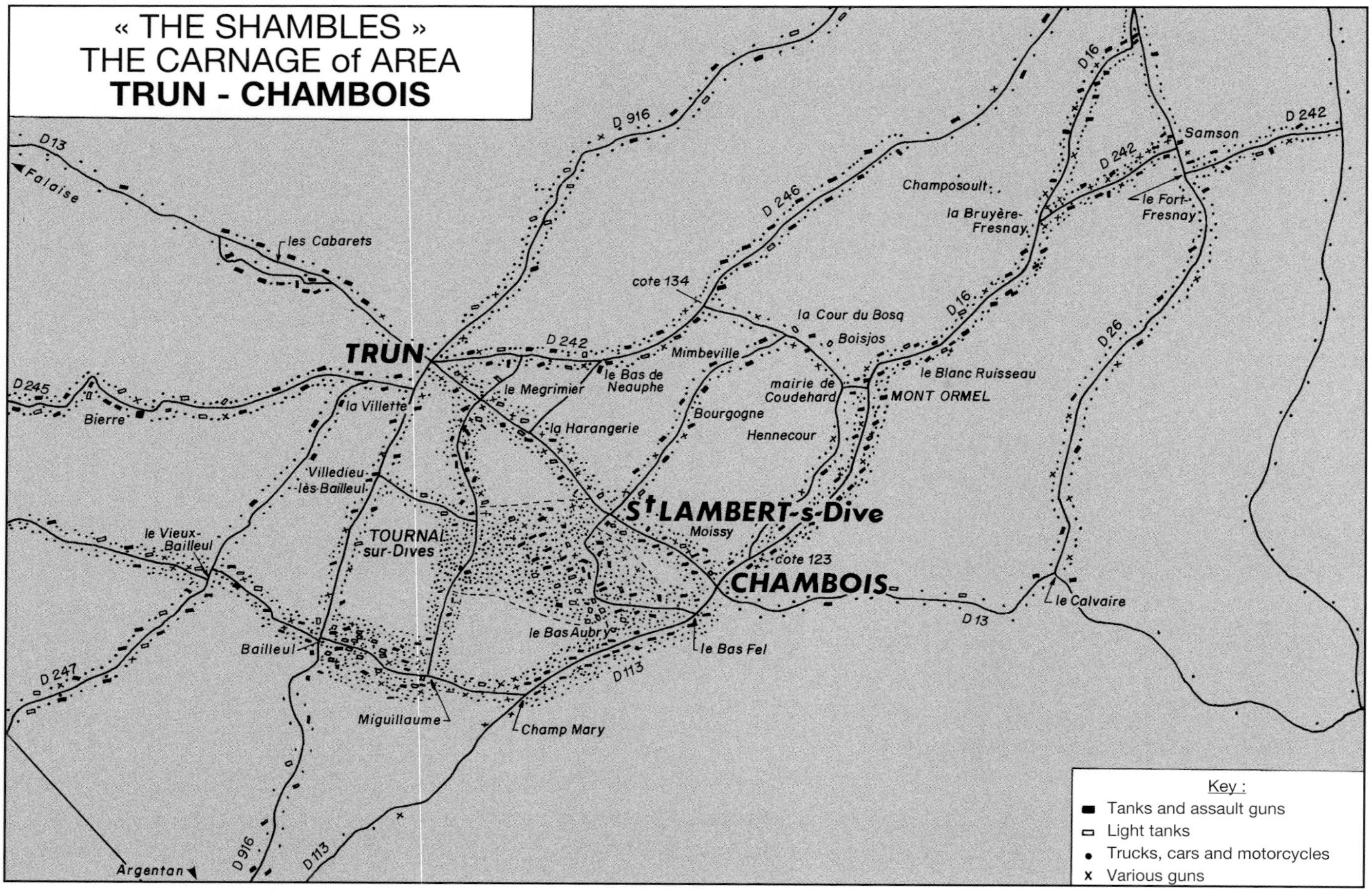

« THE SHAMBLES » THE CARNAGE of AREA **TRUN - CHAMBOIS**

Falaise
D 13
les Cabarets
D 916
D 246
Champosoult
la Bruyère-Fresnay
Samson
D 242
le Fort-Fresnay
D 16
cote 134
la Cour du Bosq
Boisjos
TRUN
D 242
Mimbeville
le Bas de Neauphe
le Megrimier
mairie de Coudehard
le Blanc Ruisseau
MONT ORMEL
D 245
Bierre
la Villette
Bourgogne
la Harangerie
Hennecour
D 26
Villedieu-lès-Bailleul
St LAMBERT-s-Dive
Moissy
le Vieux-Bailleul
TOURNAI-sur-Dives
cote 123
CHAMBOIS
le Calvaire
D 13
le Bas Aubry
le Bas Fel
Bailleul
D 113
D 247
Miguillaume
Champ Mary
Argentan
D 916
D 113

Key :
- ▬ Tanks and assault guns
- ▭ Light tanks
- • Trucks, cars and motorcycles
- x Various guns

This canadian made sketch is one fantastic document. It locates all destroyed vehicles in the Trun-Chambois sector. In one glance, one cleraly sees the jamed spots where destructions were the heaviest ; it's facing the Dive river, at the Saint Lambert mill (to the west), at the Bas-Fel (east) that most of the materiel hs been destroyed. (Heimdal, from canadian doc.)

Two german tankers burnt to death while trying to get out ot this burning Panzer IV ; a brutal and very common sight, yet rarely shown on picture, in this battle. (IWM.)

Aftermath of the Falaise-Argentan pocket

On August 21st, the Allies assess German casualties as follow : the number of Prisoner of war oscillate between 25 000 (General Montgomery's estimates) and 50 000 (according to US Army sources); 6 000 Germans have supposedly been killed or considered missing in action. These are relatively small figures considering the horrendous conditions of the german retreat. They are more or less equivalent to two divisions at full strength. On the other hand, if they did save quite a lot of men, the Germans have lost a tremendous amount of materiel ; 220 tanks, 160 guns, 700 pieces of artillery, 130 tracked vehicles (SPW), 500 motor vehicles. 1 800 dead horses must also be accounted for. Horses have paid a horrifying price. Any vehicle although riddled by bullets can still go on providing no vital parts are hit. A horse hit by one single bullet is as good as condemned to death. Only one of the five Army corps commanders has been captured. Among the 15 generals, commanding officers of full divisions, three were captured. One out of five generals made good his escape.

However, most of the figures concerning the « annihilation » of Panzer divisions have been used without verification ever since the end of the war. One can read here and there that the 2.SS-Panzer-Division

« Das Reich » was only able to save 15 tanks, 6 guns and 450 men from encirclement. In reality, 12 000 men from that division (mostly non combat troops) did reach the Seine rive. The above mentionned number only concerned one Kampfgruppe dedicated to maintain open the escape gap, while most ot the troops, rear echelon personnel and technicians, all quite valuable and competent managed to breakthrough. The 12.SS-Panzer-Division supposedly only evacuated 10 tanks, no gun and four badly mauled infantry battalions. In reality, 11 500 men did reach the Seine. Every piece of materiel not essential to the front had been pulled back. The pocket did remain open ! The heroic « Maczuga » Poles alone tried to close it. But there were not enough of them to achieve this sealing. They only acted as a «wave breaker» that inflicted heavy casualties to the oncoming Germans. They could do nothing to stop the outflanking columns of Germans overlapping the polish defences from the north and the southern flank (South of Hill 262) where the French 2nd DB was supposed to hold. Why so much exaggerations ? It was the Allies interest to built up their victory, since the war was not over yet. As for the Germans, the remorseless such as Kurt Meyer in his book « Grenadiere » tended to amplify the « heroic sacrifices» of so many fighters dying samuraï style ! As for anti-nazis, they could stress Hitler's madness. A carnage of such amplitude and the accompanying stench that lasted for monthes really struck imaginations, with thousands of soldiers who perished within a few square kilometers. But this spectacular point of view cannot hide the Allies failure. There was no Norman « Stalingrad » but rather a « Dunkirk ». The Allies shall once again a bit later during the war face in the Ardennes the same Panzer Divisions that escaped the Normandy trap. The war was to last a bit longer.

1. This picture taken August 22nd by a British war correspondant shows a SdKfz 234/3, an eight wheeled recon armored vehicle carrying a short barreled 75 mm gun. A fast vehicle, able to reach 90 km/h with an exceptionnal autonomy (100 km on plain road and 600 km cross country). This one bears the 116. Panzer-Division emblem, a styeciled greyhound. It belonged to Captain Kurt Zehner's Panzer-Aufklärung-Abteilung 116. Worth noticing is the large paint stains camo pattern. (IWM.)

2. Further on, the war correspondant also took shots of this armored Opel Maultier vehicle, with its Nebelwerfer ramp (rockets launcher). It used to belong to Werfer-Abteilung 84 whose emblem appears up front : a shell riding crow. Worth noticing a different camo pattern. (IWM.)

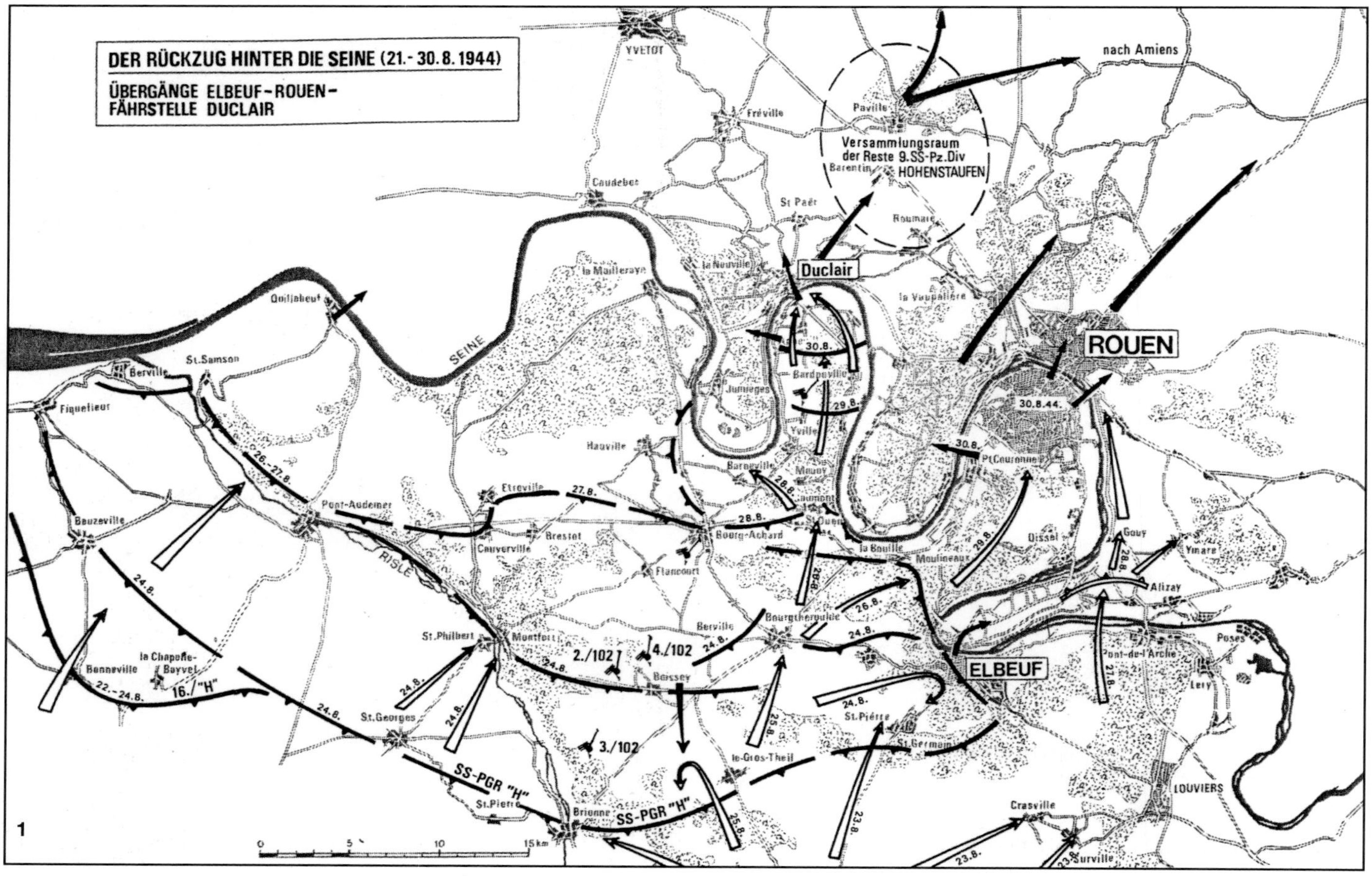

DER RÜCKZUG HINTER DIE SEINE (21.- 30. 8. 1944)

ÜBERGÄNGE ELBEUF-ROUEN-FÄHRSTELLE DUCLAIR

1

2

1. Successive withdrawal lines to the Seine, with specific mention of the Hohenstaufen pull back.The Seine crossing occured in many different spots including downstream Quillebeuf. Worth noticing here is the Risle line with its deep valley on August 24th til 27th. (H. Fürbringer/Heimdal map.)

2. The german army retreats towards the Seine. A Panther tank around Bourgtheroulde in open counry. The tank driver (of the 2.Panzer-Division or the 9. Panzer-Division) watches the sky as the tank commander assesses the situation. (BA.)

The german retreat (August 20th-30th)

Contrary to popular belief, the battle of Normandy does not end with the Falaise pocket. The Allies shall fight german troops all the way to the Seine, while trying to trap them inside a wider encirclement move, according to an american plan. As the german rear guards flee from the pocket, two american armies rush to the Seine. In the early hours of August 20th, under pouring rain, the 313th IR, 79th Infantry Division crosses the river next to Méricourt, coming out of Mantes, on a footbridge not totally blown by the Germans. Two battallions set foot on the right bank in the morning. Getting no reaction from the Germans, they operate a ferry in the afternoon. XV Corps (First US Army) thus establish a strong bridgehead near Mantes, at the edge of Upper-Normandy. On the 21st, X Corps is between Dreux and Chartres, XII Corps between Orleans and Chateaudun with the Seine up ahead from the south of Paris. On the 22nd, the Seine is crossed in Melun, where the Germans put up strong resistance. On the 23rd, they succeed in blowing up the bridge. Another failure.

In Normandy, once the pocket totally evacuated, the entire german front pulls back with British and Canadian armies hot on its heels. This withdrawal concerns several thousand men within a huge pocket sealed by one major obstacle, the Seine river. This is a huge trap, much bigger than the Falaise-Argentan pocket with no bridge intact between Rouen and the sea, except may be for the badly damaged railroad bridge in Rouen. GFM Walter Model, the desperate situations expert, try to get things organized from his 5. Panzer-Armee Command Post in Rouen. But the biggest threat is not on the retreating men with the pursuing British advancing through the Pays d'Auge. The 7th Armoured liberates Lisieux on the 23rd.

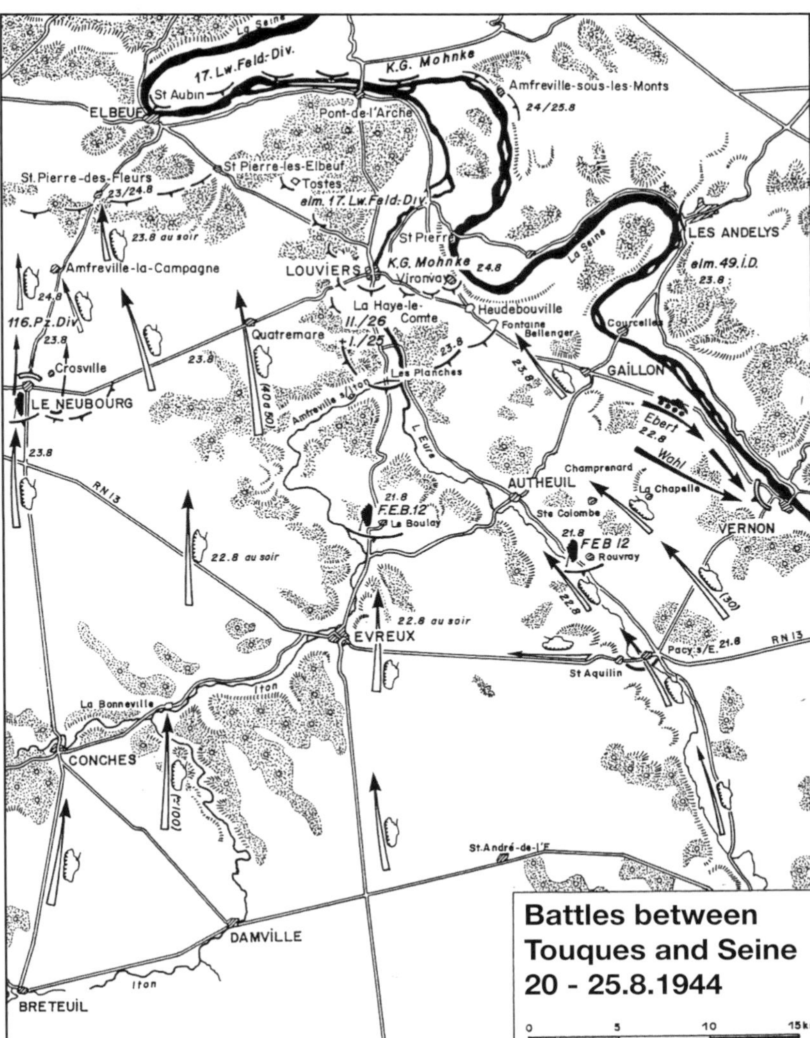

These two picturs were shot north of the Seine in Drocourt, between Mantes and Magny en Vexin (as stated on the roadsign), to the east of Normandy. This Heer unit is counter attacking the american bridghead set up by the 79th Infantry Division on August 20th. Squatting, a Captain relays his orders to two officers (a Lieutenant on the left), probably squad leaders. Moral seems good, as seen on another picture from the same reel. Further on (under) a 3,7 cm Flak is ready for action. (Photos : BA.)

On this map, note worthy are the german counter attacks lead by elements of the Hitlerjugend against the British bridgehead at Vernon. This map is connected to the previous one, at the Elbeuf level. (Heimfal map, according to H. Meyer.)

1

1 and **2.** German motorized columns, here some Waffen-SS unit, under attacks by Allied fighter bombers. These pictures might have been taken on the typical flat terrain landscape between Lisieux, Elbeuf and Bourg-Achard. However, the considerable developpment of the Allied offensive in many directions broadens the range of action of the Air force, thus rendered less efficient on the path of the german retreat in Normandie, making the withdrawal far less dramatic. 30 000 vehicles and 135 panzers will escape the Seine trap (BA.)

3. On the same newsreel, two german soldiers take a break in the retreat while vehicles burn in the backgrounds. As the Seine river approaches, the amount of vehicles waiting to cross arises, bringing up the tension.

3

The most important threat is actually east of Lisieux where British troops move up to the Seine on the american XV Corps left flank. GFM Model, assessing the danger, gathers all available panzers to stop this advance in the Evreux sector on the 22nd at nightfall, and Vernon and Louviers on the 23rd. Elbeuf remains a strongpoint upstream from Rouen to protect all the crossing points from there to the Seine estuary.

On August 24th, the vanguard of XII Corps reaches Bernay but to the north west, the First Canadian Army makes slow progress against stiff german resistance. This very same day, the II Canadian Corps crosses the Touques. On the german side, 50 000 troops are still on the southern bank of the river. On August 25th, GFM Model orders a general withdrawal ; the following night, forces located west of the Risle river are to pull back beyond that river. On August 25th and 26th, there still is a german bridgehead south of Rouen, on a Bourg-Achard, Bourgtheroulde and

4. Mots of the bridges on the Seine have been destroyed, but a large number of ferries will make the river crossing possible in many sectors, from Quillebeuf to Elbeuf, with the Hohenstaufen in Duclair as shown on map page 76. Luckily for the Germans, the Allied air superiority will not show intensively and in spite of terrible destruction scenes on the Rouen river banks, the river crossing will be an uncontested success.

Elbeuf line. From west to east, elements of the 9.SS-Panzer-Division, 10.SS-Panzer-Division and 2.SS-Panzer-Division cover the retreat. With increasing pressure, tension rises on the Seine banks. However, as indicated in Major Hans von Luck's Memoirs about the August 27th til 29th crossing, men remain calm and wait under cover their turn to load up on ferries, barges or crude rafts made out of doors. In spite of all these difficulties, the Seine crossing is a german success as confirmed by reports dated early 1945 by the RAF Bombing Analysis Unit ; The german retreat across the Seine, August 1944 : « The Seine river was no major obstacle even though all the bridges had been destroyed. » Sixty crossing points have been identified, with three boat bridges built. Overall, this reports estimates that 240 000 men made it across the river, bringing along 30 000 vehicles and 133 tanks. All men who reached the Seine crossed it successfully, along with 50% of their vehicles and 70% of their panzers. The success of the german retreat puts an end to this battle. The Allies shall fight these same troops later on, especially in the Ardennes.

Human losses

From June 6th til August 25th 1945, two millions Allied soldiers have landed in Normandy. Total Allied losses reaches 10% (206 703 men, with 124 394 Americans, 82 309 British and Canadians.) They faced a total of 740 000 german soldiers. German loses account for 240 000 casualties and 210 000 prisonners, for a total of 450 000 men. 290 000 Germans got away. Civilian casualties are heavy, about 45 000 victims including over 18 000 dead. Normandy has been torn apart by shellings and bombardments. Many cities lay in ruins, Villers Bocage suffering 86% destructions, Saint Lô 77%, Aunay sur Odon 74%, Vire 73%, Caen 73% etc...

120 000 dwellings are totally destroyed and 270 000 more are badly damaged. 43 000 hectars of farm land are temporarily out of use.

The battle field

Some parts of the battle field still carry strong images of the fightings. One can visit Rots and Bretteville l'Orgueilleuse (pages 6/7) from Caen (pages 34/35) on to Fontenay-le-Pesnel, Rauray (28/29), Evrecy and Hill 112 (42/43), Tilly and Villers-Bocage (18/19). From there on can reach Bayeux (4/5), Arromanches (26/27), Trévières and Isigny (8/9), Carentan (10/11, 20/21), Sainte-Mère-Eglise and La Fière (12/13). From this area, one moves on to Pont-l'Abbé and Saint-Sauveur-le-Vicomte (22/23) to reach Valognes and Cherbourg (24/25, 30/31). Moving down next to La Haye-du-Puits (32/33, 36/37) and Sainteny (38/39) and Saint-Lô (46/47), Coutances (54 to 57) then Mortain and Domfront (60 to 65). From there one discover the beautiful « Suisse Normande » passing by Putanges and Falaise (68/69) then Trun, Saint-Lambert and Chambois (70 to 73). Mont Ormel and its museum offers a great view of the entire pocket area.

Bibliography

Heimdal publishing has printed along a third of a century a considerable amount of books dedicated to D Day and the battle of Normandy, although some of them might be out of print. We particularly recommend *Album Memorial Normandie/Invasion Journal Pictorial* (in french and english) and also *Caen 1944, La bataille de l'Odon, Objectif Carentan, Operation Cobra, Le couloir de la mort, Objectif Falaise, La Bataille du Cotentin, Objectif Saint-Lô...* These readings can be completed by these two books in english: *Omaha Beach* and *Utah Beach*.

Destructions in the death corridor. (IWM.)

Printed on Champagne prints in France
for Heimdal Publishing, Georges Bernage, March 2017